BUSINESS CLASS

THE POWER OF PERSONAL PRESENCE

Foreword by Philip B. Miller

BUSINESS CLASS

THE POWER OF PERSONAL PRESENCE

FRP

Photography credits are listed on pages 286–287,
which constitute an extension of this copyright
page. Photographs and illustrations not otherwise
credited are © by Tom James Company.

Portrait on page 31 by Michael Shane Neal

ISBN: 978-0-615-20579-3

Edited, Designed, and Produced by

FRP

a wholly owned subsidiary of
Southwestern/Great American Inc.
P. O. Box 305142
Nashville, Tennessee 37230
800-358-0560

Text: Beth Stein
Editorial Director: Mary Cummings
Editorial Manager: Judy Jackson
Contributing Editor: Aaron Meyers
Art Direction: Steve Newman and Starletta Polster
Book Design: Phil Sankey and Karen Schmoll
Project Manager: Susan Larson
Production Supervisor: Powell Ropp

Printed in the United States of America
First Printing: 2009
20,000 copies

6   *Preface*
8   *Foreword*

10 COMPANY
STYLE
The Tom James Story

32   *Introduction*

36 BUSINESS
DRESS

38   *The Young Executive Wardrobe*
90   *The Executive's Wardrobe*
112   *Business Casual*

132 BUSINESS
CONFIDENCE

136   *Essentials*
138   *Personal Presence*
146   *Business Social*
158   *The Executive Table*
168   *Et Cetera*

178 SOCIAL DRESS

180 *Formal Occasions*
196 *Casual Occasions*
210 *What to Wear Where*

228 SOCIAL GRACES

231 *Invitations*
235 *The Good Host*
248 *After the Party*
252 *Hosting Houseguests*
254 *The Welcomed Houseguest*

262 GROOMING

286 *Photography Credits*

PREFACE

Tom James Company is a full-service clothier operating all over the United States, in Great Britain, the Netherlands, Germany, France, and Australia, with facilities in other parts of Europe and in Chile. Tom James Company was conceived in the mind of Spencer Hays.

Mr. Hays had a great interest in clothing from an early age. By 1960 he had become one of the most respected young businessmen in Nashville, Tennessee. He was taught, "As you receive from society, you should give back to society." He has always believed in giving both time and money to causes that promote the well-being of others.

By 1964, when Mr. Hays was twenty-eight years old, he had begun to think about how he could leverage his experience in direct sales and business to begin a unique custom clothing business. Spencer had a personal relationship with a banker, a life insurance agent, an accountant, a doctor, and an attorney. It seemed to him that busy professionals ought to also have a professional clothier to help them plan, build, and maintain their wardrobes.

During the course of a career, most business or professional people will make a fairly large investment in their wardrobes. Often those purchases are items bought separately without the context of a predetermined wardrobe building plan. Many of those items will just take up space in the closet but not be worn, hence wasting money.

Maybe the better you know someone the less important the way he or she dresses may seem; however, we all know that first impressions often determine whether or not we get to make a second impression. Many businesses invest a great amount of money to be in the right building. They invest in expensive space, in furniture, and in art because they value impression. First impression is not enough. The purpose of this book and Tom James Company is to help you with first impressions and lasting impressions.

Jim McEachern

DEDICATION

The Board of Directors of the Tom James Company, along with its sales professionals and employees, fondly dedicate this book to James E. McEachern, past Chief Executive Officer of the Tom James Company. For forty-two years, Jim shared with us his passion, leadership, wisdom, and friendship, and we are deeply grateful.

Tom James

FOREWORD

It has been most interesting to observe over the last fifty years, during which I was in the retail business, how the concept of business and social dressing has so dramatically evolved. I started my career as an assistant men's clothing buyer at a fine specialty store in Baltimore in the late 1950s and proceeded to the presidency of Neiman Marcus in the late '70s, the CEO of Marshall Field's in the '80s, finally becoming CEO of Saks Fifth Avenue in 1993, where I completed my retail sojourn. Throughout all these experiences I learned that good taste, personal style, and top quality are the critical factors in being well dressed and in developing a powerful personal presence.

In the '50s and through the '80s, business clothes were more formal and codified. Workplace attire was meant to convey a seriousness of purpose, and respectability, thus earning the respect and confidence of one's colleagues. One's social dress was also meant to convey a sense of gentility and good manners while, at the same time, projecting one's sense of style and care for quality. Today's office is a new world, where the previous formal standards have been relaxed, allowing more variety in dressing; however, the aforementioned principles still prevail: good taste, good quality, and style best serve the wearer and create the best impression on others. Your appearance should send an eloquent but wordless message about who you are and what you represent. Thoughtfully and tastefully selected clothes become a signifier of timeless personal qualities, such as integrity, good manners, and consideration of others.

Philip Miller, who wrote the foreword for this book, is known as one of America's premier merchants and a man of impeccable personal taste. We appreciate Mr. Miller's contribution to this book.

Good grooming and appearance seem to be self-fulfilling. We are inclined to admire the judgment and personal style of someone who is attractively dressed for a particular occasion. Conversely, we are inclined to avoid someone who has completely ignored the rules of good taste, good judgment, and appropriateness. The subtitle of this book, "The Power of Personal Presence," is the foundation for personal and professional success, and Tom James Company exists to support this concept. Spencer Hays, the founder of Tom James Company, and a principal of several other very successful enterprises, personifies the power of personal presence better than anyone I know. His meticulous grooming and charming manners are complemented by his quintessential sartorial sense. He wears finely cut suits of quality fabrics complemented by tastefully selected hand-cut shirts, beautiful ties, and elegant shoes. Spencer's commitment to quality and personal style creates a powerful personal impression complemented by his majestic personality and his belief in the power of apparel.

Business Class is about self-respect, functionality, and attention to standards. With all the options available to today's shopper, dressing tastefully for personal and professional success is more complicated than ever. While there is no longer a single right way to dress, there is still a right way to be dressed. With this guide, you can be sure of sound advice you can trust. All you have to do is turn the page.

Philip B. Miller

PANY
STYLE

The Tom James Story

Ease and charm and first impressions are only a small part of the story of how Spencer Hays started Tom James Company, Individualized Apparel Group, and Individual- ized Fabric Group before it became the world's leading manufacturer and retailer of custom men's clothing, which includes some of the most revered names in the industry. Spencer is quick to point out, though, that Tom James, IAG, and IFG were built by a team of people, not by an individual. Tom James was the seed that started this empire, a company born out of love and necessity. Its story is one of ingenuity, determination, and how a single good idea can flourish into international success.

Nine o'clock on a Tuesday morning, Spencer Hays stands to welcome a visitor into his office. The morning light filtering between mahogany blinds reveals a room richly furnished but not pretentious, sophisticated but accommodating, inviting even—much like Hays himself. Dressed impeccably on this winter morning in a beautiful dark three-piece pin-striped flannel suit complemented by a delicately striped shirt and knit tie, he smiles broadly and extends a warm, firm handshake. As he does, the right amount of crisp French cuff appears from beneath the jacket sleeve. He shows his visitor to a chair and begins engaging with benevolent questions meant to make another feel at home. He jokes a little at his own expense, laughs easily. It is immediately obvious how this man from humble Oklahoma roots founded Tom James Company, now an international clothing group that for forty years has helped business executives and professionals craft successful impressions. He is a master at it.

Ease and charm and first impressions are only a small part of the story of how Spencer Hays started Tom James Company, Individualized Apparel Group, and Individualized Fabric Group before it became the world's leading manufacturer and retailer of custom men's clothing, which includes some of the most revered names in the industry. Spencer is quick to point out, though, that Tom James, IAG, and IFG were built by a team of people, not by an individual. Tom James was the seed that started this empire, a company born out of love and necessity. Its story is one of ingenuity, determination, and how a single good idea can flourish into international success.

It is also a story of intriguing dichotomies. While Tom James' business may be dressing the body, the company's philosophy focuses more on the heart. Founded on time-honored principles that stress personal integrity, sharing, encouraging one another, the power of positive thinking, loyalty, individual initiative, and tenacity, the company has steadily put people development ahead of profits. It was started in 1966 not by an exclusive group of veteran clothing industry executives, but—in Hays' own words—"a bunch of farm boys," smart, character-driven, dedicated farm boys who also happened to hold degrees in agriculture, business, economics, education, engineering, and law. The company's simple, grassroots approach—along with a steadfast commitment to quality products and people—has proven itself. In just forty years, Tom James has expanded from a homegrown, four-man operation to become the international trademark for custom men's clothing, with offices in thirty-nine states, England, Scotland, France, Germany, Holland, Chile, Australia, and beyond.

In the beginning . . .

Spencer Hays always loved beautiful clothing. He admired the fine clothes he would see at the "clean and press shop" in his hometown of Gainesville, Texas. He worked there as a young boy to help make ends meet. His maternal grandmother—the woman who helped raise him after his father left—did tailoring and alterations for the local department store. Mary Moore would bring home the finest Ardmore had to offer in the way of upscale fashion. From her, Hays learned the value of a well-executed hand stitch, along with even more valuable lessons on life. Her profound influence set him on his path to success and still remains a force in his life. When Hays established a generous relief fund in the 1980s to help any employee in an emergency, he named it the Mary Moore Foundation in her memory.

Before Hays was even out of grade school, he began crafting his personal style. "I was the odd guy who wore a sports jacket to school when I was in the eighth grade," Hays remembers, amused at the thought of his dandy appearance in rural Texas. How that love of clothing would eventually become a direct-sales business began its circuitous route when he was recruited out of Gainesville to Texas Christian University on a basketball scholarship.

> *"I was the odd guy who wore a sports jacket to school when I was in the eighth grade."*

"I thought we could help people—
  doctors, lawyers, businesspeople—
project a more professional image
  through trained salespeople who could
help their clients by explaining the advantages
  of the right colors, patterns, fabrics,
  and body styles.
  These salespeople would become
  familiar with the needs of their clients
and help them plan, build, and maintain
  their wardrobes in order to project that
professional image while making the most
  of their investment in their wardrobes.
  These Tom James Company salespeople
would also save their clients time and
  add convenience to the shopping
experience by meeting with their clients
  in their own offices or homes."

Three schools offered him athletic scholarships that year, but he chose TCU because it was thirty miles from his girlfriend, Marlene, now his wife of more than fifty years.

During his freshman year at TCU, recruiters from Southwestern Publishing Company visited the campus looking for summer salespeople. The established Nashville, Tennessee-based company employed students from all over the country each summer to sell Bibles, dictionaries, and cookbooks door-to-door in rural areas. Some of them made thousands of dollars, a lot of money at the time. To a poor college kid like Hays, the idea sounded promising. He signed on and started as soon as school was out that summer.

"Spencer started slowly, but by the end of his first summer he was the #1 first year salesman," says Robert Sherrer, now Chairman of the Board of Tom James Company and, like many Tom James executives, a former Southwestern summer book salesman. "Spencer also became the #1 second, third, and fourth summer salesman, and recruited a large number of students from TCU and several other colleges to sell with him during those second, third, and fourth summers."

After Hays graduated from college in 1959, he moved to Nashville to work full-time for Southwestern. By the mid-1960s he had risen to the top of the company. As Southwestern flourished, he was bothered that Southwestern trained a force of top-notch salespeople during the summers, but had no way of retaining these talented young men (and, by this time, women) in sales once they graduated. Ever the entrepreneur, he began to figure out some way to capitalize on this resource. His love of fine clothes, coupled with the increased demands on his time, gave him an idea: Why couldn't custom clothing be sold to busy executives on a direct sales basis?

The more he thought about the concept, the more he liked it. He could see advantages not only of saving the customer time, but also how such a business could offer a whole new level of personalized service and smart wardrobe building.

"After moving to Nashville in 1960, the first suit I bought, I bought from a department store from someone who hardly knew my name, much less would remember what I bought last year or the year before or tell me what suit I should buy next," Hays says. "I thought we could help people—doctors, lawyers, businesspeople—project a more professional image through trained salespeople who could help their clients by explaining the advantages of the right colors, patterns, fabrics, and body styles. These salespeople would become familiar with the needs of their clients and help them plan, build, and maintain their wardrobes in order to project that professional image while making the most of their investment in their wardrobes. These Tom James Company salespeople would also save their clients time and add convenience to the shopping experience by meeting with their clients in their own offices or homes."

So in 1966, Hays—then just thirty—approached a few select people about joining him in his new clothing venture. One of them was Jim McEachern, whom he had met selling books back in the mid-1950s.

> *He could see advantages... how such a business could offer a whole new level of personalized service and smart wardrobe building.*

"When Spencer contacted me about the new company, I was living in Fort Worth," says McEachern, who headed Tom James for more than thirty years and has only recently retired to spend more time with family. "He didn't even tell me what business he was going to start, and I didn't care because I had developed a lot of respect for him. I believed in him and his business philosophy. Even now, after working with Spencer for more than forty years, I've never known anyone with whom I'd prefer to work." Another fellow Hays called upon was Tom James. Tom's father, Bronco James, had been his Sunday School teacher back in Ardmore and a positive influence on his young life. Son Tom had worked in a men's fine clothing store and had just graduated from the University of Oklahoma law school. When Hays approached him, he, too, was interested.

"We named the company for him because I wanted something that sounded English," Hays says. "English fashion was the big thing then. The Italians hadn't yet come on the scene."

Hays then contracted with English American Tailoring Company in Maryland to make Tom James' custom suits and with Individualized Shirt Company in New Jersey for shirts. Both companies were Genesco holdings and known for high-end quality products. We later bought both companies in order to be able to control our quality and delivery. Through these resources, Tom James could also offer sportswear—sports coats, trousers, and patterned shirts—for social wear. All the essentials were in place.

Hays launched the Tom James operation in Nashville. After a year in Nashville, McEachern moved to Atlanta to open the second Tom James location. Memphis and Dallas debuted shortly thereafter. Tom James opened storefronts in each of these cities to complement the direct sales approach. The idea was to call on customers in person and set up appointments for them to come into the store for professional fitting, fabric selection, and to coordinate accessories like neckties.

One of Hays' favorite mantras came from Clement Stone, which says, "You can't teach what you don't know, and you can't lead where you won't go." He began knocking on doors inside one of Nashville's few skyscrapers to see if he could sell clothing to executives. Although now well established in the Nashville business community as a leader at Southwestern, he didn't hesitate to resume the door-to-door sales role again. He called on friends and strangers to peddle his new idea.

Hays understood that the Tom James Company's strengths were personal service and the ability to package the professional properly for any occasion, but he wasn't sure how to best present these concepts so men would listen. Each day, he would make calls and try to refine the business approach. Each night, he would return to Southwestern to evaluate what worked and what didn't.

"You can't teach what you don't know, and you can't lead where you won't go."

"I tried to figure out what caused people to want to let me see them even if they had never met me," he says. "That's where I came upon the idea of getting clients to make referrals. Now we ask for referrals at every sale."

Another aspect of the business that became clear as he and others sought to refine their approach was the Tom James advantage of going to clients instead of having clients come to them.

"I had a customer who said, 'You've got my measurements. Why don't you just bring the fabrics to my office?' I did, and he bought three suits," McEachern recalls. "That gave me an idea, so I started telling all my clients that I could take the fabrics to their offices for their selection. In June 1967, I sold seventy-two suits, all in customers' offices. That began to change our approach."

The company continued to grow at a steady rate. In 1967, the first full year clothing was actually sold, sales totaled approximately $165,000. Jim McEachern set an ambitious goal of growing the company to $100 million in sales by doubling its figures every two to three years. "By the end of 1967 I had seen that we could develop a happy clientele by delighting them with our products and service, so growing to $100 million in sales seemed like a natural consequence," McEachern says. "I had come to believe that business and professional people would buy from us if they developed confidence in us as individuals, in our company, and in our products. The first purchase often depends on a good presentation. Repeat purchases depend upon their satisfaction with our products and personal service."

Sales were $400,000 in 1968, $900,000 in 1969, and $1.3 million in 1970. By the end of 1970, Tom James had seven locations. Lindy Watkins, Aaron Meyers, and Robert Sherrer had all joined the team after college summers selling books. All three would spend their careers with Tom James.

Most business and professional people recognize that an investment in their wardrobe and appearance is an investment in their future.

The company's unique culture, people-oriented philosophy, and growing success attracted the attention of ambitious, career-minded salespeople from across the country.

But just two years after Hays started Tom James, the men who owned Southwestern—Fred Landers and Dortch Oldham—decided to sell the entire company to Times-Mirror Company, at that time a powerful media conglomerate of magazines and newspapers, including the prestigious *Los Angeles Times*. When Al Casey, CEO of Times-Mirror, asked Hays to stay on as president of Southwestern, he agreed, provided he could also run his new business on the side.

"I didn't want to see it closed down," Hays says. "I didn't want to do that to all the people who were in the business. I made a deal with Times-Mirror that allowed me to be CEO of Southwestern, but also keep Tom James going."

In 1982 Spencer Hays bought Southwestern back from Times-Mirror. By then, the Tom James concept had been solidified and the business was flourishing. All Tom James retail stores had been closed in favor of offices that served as home base between sales calls. Salespeople had graduated from carrying big bolts of fabric to clients' offices to carrying a full line of swatches. The art of measuring and fitting for custom clothing became part of the sales training, and Tom James associates could now execute the entire transaction on the client's turf. They provided the entire wardrobe, from suits and shirts to shoes, neckties, sports coats, and casual clothing to formalwear. Tom James' prime selling points spoke for themselves: convenience that stemmed from going to the customer, a larger selection than any retail establishment could stock, customizing for each client, and, without real estate, lower operating expenses that allowed us to give better value and quality to our customers than our competitors could offer.

One of our philosophies is to delight our clients. When buying from a Tom James person, you are buying from an owner. Our mission for customers is to make sure they receive excellent service and advice regarding their wardrobe with quality and value, so they are properly attired for every situation. That's part of the mission statement. We need to know what type of meetings they go to, where they go, who they're with. If they feel a whole lot better about themselves because of the way they look, our mission is accomplished. We help our clients select, balance, coordinate, and maintain their wardrobes, so they can be confident that they are perfectly attired for every occasion.

This formula worked well, and the business attracted not only clients, but more and more top salespeople. As predicted at the outset, many of them came from Southwestern summer book sales. The company's unique culture, people-oriented philosophy, and growing success attracted the attention of ambitious, career-minded salespeople from across the country.

Among the primary reasons men and women buy their clothing from Tom James Company are

- They love the products.
- They receive great value.
- They like the convenience of shopping in their own offices.
- They benefit from the time they save because they don't have to go to a store.
- They like the person who serves them.
- They receive great ideas from their Tom James professional.
- They can buy with confidence.
- Tom James is a full-service clothier.

They keep buying from Tom James Company for the same reasons. Many clients like Tom James Company so well they recommend it to their friends.

This is an archival book of Holland & Sherry, the world's greatest cloth merchant.

Expansion . . .

Spencer Hays understood that salespeople could only be successful if the product was first-class. Frustrations with timely delivery on custom clothing made it clear that to fulfill its founder's vision for service, Tom James would need better control over suppliers. So, we did the only logical thing we could. We bought them to gain control over quality and the time it takes for delivery.

The marked improvement put Tom James on a path to acquire more manufacturers to supply their customers. Hays eventually formed Individualized Apparel Group (IAG) as an umbrella for these growing manufacturing interests. Savvy purchases put him in a position not only to serve Tom James but also to become a leader in the wholesale business for the global retail market. Since then, Tom James has acquired Oxxford Clothes, H. Freeman, Gitman Brothers, Corbin Trousers, Franklin Clothing, Kenneth Gordon Shirts, Measure Up Custom Shirtmakers, Ltd., Y'Apre Cravats, and Brown & Church Neckwear. Before long, IAG holdings were manufacturing for many of menswear's most revered labels: Saks Fifth Avenue, Neiman-Marcus, Nordstrom, Dillards, Bergdorf Goodman, Larrimors, Louis of Boston, Mitchells, Richards, Wilkes Bashford, Paul Stuart, Mr. Ooley's, Syd Jerome, Maus and Hoffman, Kilgore Trout, Carroll & Co., Parsow's, Hunt Club, Sam Cavuto, Stanley Korshak, James Davis, Levy's, and Culwell's, just to name a few. The Individualized Fabric Group was formed to acquire Holland & Sherry Ltd., of Peebles, Scotland, merchandiser of some of the world's finest cloths since 1836, and Clissold.

The addition of IAG also allowed Tom James to easily add a new dimension to its business. Since Tom James had already established a base with executives in the big corner offices, the company began looking toward the younger men and women at the firms and businesses they called on. These people also needed to look professional, but weren't ready to delve into custom prices. With all these manufacturing resources at Tom James' disposal, it was a natural for its salespeople to begin offering less expensive ready-made clothing as well. As with the custom

business, they were able to offer higher quality at better prices than the competition, not to mention the Tom James personalized service at no added cost. This opened up a whole new customer base for the company, and sales continued to increase. Owning both the manufacturing and retail enables Tom James to enhance the value of its products and service to its clients.

A different kind of company . . .

If you said that perfecting the direct-sales custom clothing business and becoming a global player in the retail, wholesale, and manufacture of fine clothing were the keys to the success of Tom James, IAG, and IFG, you would be politely, but firmly, corrected by those in the company. From Spencer Hays on down, Tom James associates will tell you the company's greatest asset is not its holdings, but its people.

Perhaps Hays' most famous philosophy—the one echoed verbatim by many of his associates—is, "You don't build a successful company; you build successful people and they build the company." This philosophy permeates Tom James, from how clients are treated to making salespeople shareholders to structuring the sales force so each salesperson has unlimited opportunity to succeed. First, individuals are trained and prove themselves as sellers who can build a satisfied clientele. Then they begin recruiting other sellers to be on their "team." Team leaders are then responsible for training and motivating their team members to become successful, realizing they must do whatever it takes to delight each client. This compound approach allows even young salespeople to realize significant gains within the first few years and to expect those gains to rise exponentially in the future.

"Spencer wanted to build a company where people could increase their net worth," says Ash Deshmukh, a Senior Vice President of Tom James who joined the company in 1974. "The path to success in Tom James is you develop a great clientele, and then you recruit others and bring them into the business and teach them how to do what you do. By developing others, you build an organization. Ultimately, one who builds an organization reaps the greatest rewards."

From the beginning the company leadership has believed that Tom James people who see an unlimited opportunity for themselves and who have ownership will naturally respect the value of providing clients the best products and service for their investment in their wardrobes. Career-minded Tom James people naturally respect the good sense of their customers.

Employees also appreciate the absence of politics within Tom James and the lack of obstacles to personal success. The hierarchy is such that only a handful of Tom James' executives hold exclusively administrative positions. Most continue to sell and help other salespeople. "It's strictly a performance-based business," says Deshmukh.

> *"You don't build a successful company; you build successful people and they build the company."*

What does make a difference is persistence and hard work. No one at Tom James will say direct sales is an easy business. It takes a special individual to maintain a successful pace day after day and to endure a lot of personal rejection in the process. This kind of stress creates turnover. But those at the top have made it their business to take care of salespeople and equip each with a personal motivation and strategies for achieving at a high level. In sales meetings, Tom James associates don't talk just about selling finely tailored custom clothing. Instead, they focus on the things they want to achieve in their lives and how to reach those goals. From the moment salespeople join Tom James, they are groomed to find the best in themselves and realize untapped potential.

"If a person doesn't know what he wants in life, it's difficult to talk about clothing, deliveries, and so on," says Sergio Casalena, Tom James CEO and one of the many company executives who did not sell for Southwestern. "What they want doesn't have to be monetary. Some talk about having balance in their personal and family life. Whatever it is, they have to believe they can get it here."

"Spencer is a master at connecting you to what you do each day and to something that's important to you," according to President Bob Sherrer. "Maybe it's an item or a trip you want; maybe it's helping you become the kind of person you want to become."

For many customers, Tom James' contribution to their lives is the time saved and the convenience of having the salesperson come to the office or home. The most comfortable place to do business is often one's own office.

Aaron Meyers adds, "Our job is to help our salespeople and clients get a bigger 'bite out of life.' Everyone wants more happiness and success."

Knowing this, it's no surprise that those in the Tom James organization often talk of each other as family.

"We take a lot of pains to hire and train," Deshmukh says. "We take on new salespeople to raise them. They're like our children. We work with them under any situation. It's very difficult to get fired here, unless you have integrity issues. Our whole principle is based on the belief that all people have potential for greatness within them. Our job is to bring that out. Even in the early years when the company lost money, we knew we had to take care of our people. Tom James' business philosophy is geared toward long-term growth, not short-term success. We stood by people when the going was tough. We really mean people are our greatest asset."

> *"Spencer is a master at connecting you to what you do each day and to something that's important to you. Maybe it's an item or a trip you want; maybe it's helping you become the kind of person you want to become."*

Philosophy of Our Businesses
Compiled by Spencer Hays
And His Business Associates

- We believe in excellence and make it a habit.
- We believe that we cannot build a business; we build people and people build the business. We put great emphasis on creating an atmosphere in which people can take their God-given talents, skills, and capabilities and have fun achieving and accomplishing.
- We believe that we will do what it takes to delight our customers.
- We believe that we are in business to serve our customers, and the way to maintain customers is to always give more value than we charge for.
- We believe that management's first responsibility is to run the company in such a way that it makes money. If not, how can the company stay in business and continue giving customers the good quality products they want?
- We believe it is management's responsibility to guarantee every worker in our business job security, and the only way we can do that is to run the company in such a way that we make money. The only way a company can make money is to grow its sales. If a company's sales stay the same, since expenses are going up every year, it makes less money. The only way a company can grow its profits is to grow its sales.
- We believe in taking from profit each year and putting that back into the business, enabling us to give even better products and services to our customers.
- We have a profit-sharing plan as part of our business. We believe it is our responsibility to give each employee the opportunity to retire with dignity and self-respect.
- All of the key people within our companies own part of the business. They have an owner's viewpoint and perspective. Therefore, they will always give the very best quality and service and remember that the customer is first.
- Waste leads to want, so we work very hard not to squander money. This means we have more money to spend on better services and products for our customers.
- We believe in the importance of a wholesome and good attitude. If we think we can, we can. We can, we will, we are going to excel and succeed.
- There are two types of people in this world—one looks for a way, the other looks for an excuse. It doesn't take guts, gumption, or determination to find an excuse; anybody can locate one. It takes a quality person to find a way over, under, around, or right through any obstacle that stands in the way.
- A lot of people are talkers. They talk about all the things they can do, but sometimes they don't do them. My grandmother always said, "Don't judge people by what they say; judge them by what they do." We should place our worth, not on what we think we can do, but on what we actually do.
- The people who are coming up under a manager are always going to notice the way that manager expresses himself/herself. If a manager gives credit and praise to peers and the people over him/her, then the people coming up under that manager will feel the same way. If a manager expresses trust of peers and the people over him/her, the people coming up under that manager will feel the same way. If a manager shows appreciation for peers and the people over him/her, the

people coming up under that manager will feel the same. The right example is so important. Also, our customers will feel about us the way we feel about our peers and the people over us.
- Never be critical of anyone to someone else. If we say something to someone for the purpose of helping a person, it should be said only to the people who can actually have an influence on the person we are talking about.
- We don't want to be right; we want to be for what is right.
- We are not important, but what we do is important. We have seen a few men and women do extremely well over a long period of time, and we have seen a lot of people do well for a short period of time, and then fail. The people who do well over a long period of time always think of what they are trying to achieve as being more important than themselves. If we make ourselves more important than the things we are trying to achieve, we become petty and selfish, and we fail.
- Today is the day and now is the time to achieve and accomplish. Get the order today. Make the sale today.
- The difficult can be done right away; the impossible takes just a little longer.
- We believe in the importance of enthusiasm. If we act enthusiastic, we will become enthusiastic. William James, a great Harvard psychologist, discovered that action goes before feeling. We can control and regulate our feelings by controlling and regulating our actions. If we act a certain way, we begin to feel that way. Action goes before feeling.
- Never be part of the problem; be part of the solution to the problem. People like this are motivational and inspiring to others.
- All problems can be solved within five feet of where they happen, not miles away in an office.
- Little people get upset over little things; big people don't. Unfortunately, a lot of people go through their entire lives getting upset and spending a lot of time and energy on incidental things that don't make a bit of difference.
- Form the habit of doing things failures don't like to do. Failures don't like to plan in advance. They don't like to call and make their appointments in advance. They don't like to see a certain number of new people every day. They don't like to confront people about actions that are not consistent with their goals.
- We live in an age of intellectual giants and emotional midgets. We can put a man on the moon and bring him back, but we can't control ourselves and overcome our emotions enough to overcome the fear of failure and the fear of rejection. Many times we are so afraid we can't do something that we don't even attempt it.
- The way to overcome the fear of rejection is to make the call! The way to overcome the fear of failure is to keep figuring out better and better ways of doing our job. If we don't succeed at first, we keep trying and trying.
- There is no limit to what can be accomplished, if we don't care about who gets the credit.
- Set high goals, give good self-talk, and be accountable.
- What we are someday going to be, we are now becoming.
- We are all part of a team. It takes many people doing many different things to build a great company—no one can do it alone.
- Real success is doing our best.

He seeks to reinforce character in every employee, as evidenced in the official "Tom James Company Business Philosophy." This is a document containing twenty-eight points given to every employee. Some points address company strategy, like Number 7: *"We believe strongly in taking from profit each year and putting that back into the business, enabling us to give even better products and services to our customers."* But more resemble passages from an inspirational self-help book. Number 11: *"We always want to promote the philosophy of a wholesome and good attitude. 'If you think you can, you can.' A successful person says, 'I can, I will, I am going to excel and succeed.' A successful person realizes the difficult can be done right away; the impossible takes just a little longer."* Or Number 15: *"We always want to promote never being critical of anyone to someone else."* Number 17: *"We always want to promote the philosophy of, 'I am not important, but what I do is important.' If we do this, then we won't be consumed with our own importance."* Number 22: *"Little people get upset over little things; big people don't."*

For the past forty years, according to Todd Browne, every Tom James sales professional has also been taught the principles from the classic bestseller *How to Win Friends and Influence People*, written by Dale Carnegie. The book has been published in thirty-eight languages with more than fifty million copies in print.

"This book has been the foundation of our sales and leadership training to help our people grow and improve their personal skills," he says.

"When you are inspired by some great purpose, some extraordinary project, all your thoughts break their bounds. Your mind transcends limitations, your consciousness expands in every direction, and you find yourself in a new, great, and wonderful world."

Bob Sherrer recalls another of Spencer's favorite sayings: "Spencer told me, and I carried this on a 3x5 card for years, 'Tie yourself to principles, appreciate people, and enjoy things.' If you tie yourself to principles, you'll forgive others when they disappoint you.'"

Some of Hays' philosophical sayings come from his grandmother. Some were gifts from his days as a Southwestern salesman, especially from his mentor there, Fred Landers. Some have come from famous leaders and authors; some are original. His sources were always diverse. The following selection of Hays' often-quoted sayings on the importance of self-talk and controlling one's own thinking—fundamental topics at Tom James— prove that.

"When you are inspired by some great purpose, some extraordinary project, all your thoughts break their bounds. Your mind transcends limitations, your consciousness expands in every direction, and you find yourself in a new, great, and wonderful world. Dormant forces, faculties, and talents become alive, and you discover yourself to be a greater person by far than you ever dreamed yourself to be."

—Patanjali

"Our life is what our thoughts make it."

—Marcus Aurelius

"As a man thinketh in his heart so is he."

—Proverbs 23:7

"The aphorism, 'As a man thinketh in his heart so is he,' not only embraces the whole of a man's being, but is so comprehensive as to reach out to every condition and circumstance of his life. A man is literally what he thinks."

—James Allen

As all young Southwestern book salesmen did, Hays carried notecards in his pocket with some of these affirmations on them. To psych himself up before each call, he would pull out a notecard to read something like, *"Every day in every way by the grace of God I am becoming better and better."* He still begins each day early by saying out loud five to ten times, "I feel healthy, I feel happy, I feel terrific."

"By the time I do that, I feel better, even if my back hurts—or whatever," he says with a smile. "While I shave, I say, 'There are two types of persons: the one who finds a way and the one who finds an excuse.' While I tie my tie, I say over and over, 'Today is the day, now is the time.'

"Of course, my wife makes me close the door while all this is going on."

Examples from Carnegie's book that have influenced the growth of Tom James:

- Don't criticize, condemn, or complain.
- Give honest, sincere appreciation.
- Become genuinely interested in other people.
- Smile.
- Remember that a person's name is to that person the sweetest and most important sound in any language.
- Be a good listener. Encourage others to talk about themselves.
- Make the other person feel important and do it sincerely.
- The only way to get the best of an argument is to avoid it.
- Begin with praise and honest appreciation.
- Let the other person save face.
- Once a decision is reached, act!
- Use the law of averages to outlaw your worries.
- Fill your mind with thoughts of peace, courage, health, and hope.
- Count your blessings, not your troubles.

"OUR LIFE IS WHAT OUR THOUGHTS MAKE IT."

—Marcus Aurelius

Some of Hays'
philosophical sayings
come from his grandmother.
Some were gifts from his days as a
Southwestern salesman, especially
from his mentor there, Fred Landers.
Some have come from famous leaders
and authors; some are original.
His sources were always diverse.

"AS A MAN THINKETH IN HIS HEART SO IS HE."

—Proverbs 23:7

"Spencer is the first person I knew who connected activity to affirmation," Sherrer says, remembering his early days at Tom James. "I was afraid not to do it."

Hays is not the only senior Tom James executive whose wisdom and leadership have had a profound impact on many within the company. In conversations about who has been both influential and inspirational, Jim McEachern's name surfaces frequently.

"When I was a very young man, my father taught me, 'Son, if you find a turtle on top of a fencepost, you can be sure it didn't get there by itself.'" Meyers says. "This principle certainly applies to me and my Tom James career, as many men have influenced my success. Jim McEachern is one of these very influential leaders in our company. When I moved to Atlanta in the autumn of 1967, I was very fortunate to begin my career working at Tom James with Jim as my leader. I have learned many things from Jim and his outstanding leadership, but most of all I appreciate his challenge to me to grow as a leader. He believed in me and treated me as the person I could become rather than how I saw myself."

McEachern set forth his own set of principles or guidelines for Tom James salespeople, titled "The Most Important Things I Can Do as a Tom James Leader."

1. Make people feel appreciated.
2. Make people feel that they belong.
3. Make people feel that what they do is important . . . that they count, that they make a difference.
4. Help people develop a vision for what they can become, can achieve, can do, and can have.
5. Help people develop specific goals with monetary values and plans.
6. Help people face and overcome fears, doubt, and regrets.
7. Help people develop competency relating to sales, products, and technical aspects of our business.
8. Make sure that people know that you believe in them.

All of these things need to be done over and over again . . . forever. "The better Tom James people feel about themselves and their opportunity in our company, the better they serve their customers," says McEachern.

All of this positive thinking and reinforcement is still part of daily life for Tom James employees today. They can recite many of McEachern's and Hays' favorite affirmations by heart, and they frequently quote these as motivation to team members during regular communications.

All of this positive thinking and reinforcement is still part of daily life for Tom James employees today. They can recite many of McEachern's and Hays' favorite affirmations by heart, and they frequently quote these as motivation to team members during regular communications.

But the hype stops when salespeople call on clients. Whatever image one might have of most salespeople would likely be shattered by the Tom James salesman. They understand that their clients are established professionals who don't appreciate a hustle. The sales approach is non-manipulative, casual, and without pressure. Many of the salespeople have been calling on certain clients for so many years that the sales calls are more like social calls. True friendships have developed. The conversation is as much about family members, golf games, and travel plans as about clothing. That is part of the reason 85 percent of Tom James' business is from repeat customers. This growth would be impossible without career-oriented people who genuinely care about pleasing customers. Happy customers become repeat buyers and refer the company to their friends.

The future . . .

The year 2006 marked Tom James' fortieth anniversary. The company arrived at this milestone as three divisions: Tom James Retail, selling clothing directly to the customer, the Individualized Apparel Group, which handles all the manufacturing for Tom James and sells to other retailers, and the Individualized Fabric Group. There are now one hundred twenty Tom James sales offices in the U.S., England, Holland, France, Australia, and Germany. There are also eight domestic manufacturing facilities making suits, trousers, shirts, and ties; a fabric merchandiser, Holland & Sherry, providing the world's finest fabrics to Tom James and other fine clothing makers; and, most recently, a fabric mill in Tome, Chile, making very fine Super 100s to 180s worsted wool and linen fabric for Tom James' retail and other clothing manufacturing customers. Tom James employs 2,665 people worldwide, with approximately five hundred of them in direct sales and wardrobe planning for top professionals and business executives.

"We are very proud of the fact that in recent years, 30 percent of our salespeople earned six figures, and the percentage is growing," says Ash Deshmukh. "Not many direct sales companies can say that."

In 1992 the goal of $100,000,000 in annual sales was achieved. The annual growth rate from 1967 through 1992 was almost 30 percent. Now Tom James Company is on the way to $1,000,000,000 in annual sales. "The key factor in the sales growth has been a team of people who are passionate about delighting customers with our products and service. We believe we are in business to serve our customers and the way to do that is to offer more value than we charge for. We will do whatever it takes to delight our customers," is the way Mr. Sherrer describes the reason for the consistent growth of Tom James Company.

Mr. Sherrer also says, "The people in Tom James Company who serve clients are also owners of our business, so they have a vested interest in delighting our clients. As anyone will, we do make mistakes, but we know that it is our responsibility to bring every transaction to a happy conclusion for our clients."

"Our expansion into the United Kingdom, Europe, and Australia has doubled our retail and manufacturing sales potential," says Paul Copp. "We have found that businessmen all over the world appreciate the professional wardrobe planning and quality products that Tom James has become known for over the past forty years."

These figures speak for themselves and for why so many men placed confidence in Spencer Hays when he came to them forty years ago with an unusual idea about direct selling custom clothing.

Clothing is the most personal of products that most people buy because it reflects the way we see ourselves. Buying from Tom James Company means you are buying from a person who is committed to understanding how each customer wants to dress. Furthermore, Tom James Company offers such a large selection that the unique taste of each customer can easily be fulfilled.

CEO Casalena says, "We help our customers build, balance, coordinate, and maintain their wardrobes, so they can be perfectly attired for any occasion they find themselves in, whether it be business, casual, formal, or social."

According to Joe Blair, President of IAG, the manufacturing and wholesale part of the Tom James Company, "A good first impression often determines whether or not a person gets the opportunity to prove himself to a potential client, so an investment in our wardrobes is an investment in our future. Attention to detail in the way we dress often indicates attention to detail in our work."

When asked if, of all his affirmations, quotations, and principles, there is one favorite, Hays smiles. "It comes from my grandmother," he says. Of course. She was quoting Edwin Markham: "THERE IS A DESTINY THAT MAKES US BROTHERS; NONE GOES HIS WAY ALONE. WHAT YOU PUT INTO THE LIVES OF OTHERS, COMES BACK INTO YOUR OWN."

Casalena believes Tom James' direct sales approach has had a huge impact on the upscale clothing business in general. "In Charlotte alone, we have fifteen people calling on customers and prospective customers," he says. "It made those customers think about custom clothing even if they didn't buy. The industry has benefited tremendously by our making people aware of their attire. We're the only one talking about it. Everyone else puts it in print. But we're talking about it, and our message is really clear." Doctors, attorneys, and accountants work one-on-one with their clients. It makes sense that clothiers do the same thing. That is what Tom James Company is about.

One of the books Tom James salespeople know well is *Good to Great* by Jim Collins. In that book, Collins discusses the "hedgehog principle" that says, basically, decide what you're good at and stick to it. Chairman Bob Sherrer refers to this principle when he says, "We're best at direct sales. We have such intense focus on helping people decide what they want. We're positively the best in the world at that."

Tom James' people aren't the only ones doling out compliments. The company's unique approach to custom clothing has been featured in many major metropolitan daily newspapers and magazines like *Forbes*. Hays lands annually on menswear industry trade paper *DNR*'s "Power 100," a listing of the most powerful people in menswear.

Even though Tom James continues to grow at an impressive clip into the twenty-first century as a thoroughly modern retail, wholesale, and manufacturing conglomerate, the company's standards and traditional values will not change. The sales force may expand and may be doing business in a multiplicity of languages, but the old-fashioned tenets of success and the company's emphasis on people remain steadfast. Despite the fact that Spencer Hays and many of those who work with him now find themselves surrounded by enviable success, their conversation continually comes back to simple principles. There is little pretense here. Even among the fine art and rich appointments of Hays' homes in Nashville and New York, it is easy to still find the man who sat in his grandmother's Ardmore, Oklahoma, kitchen soaking up lessons in life. Those lessons echo down through the ranks at Tom James and serve it well.

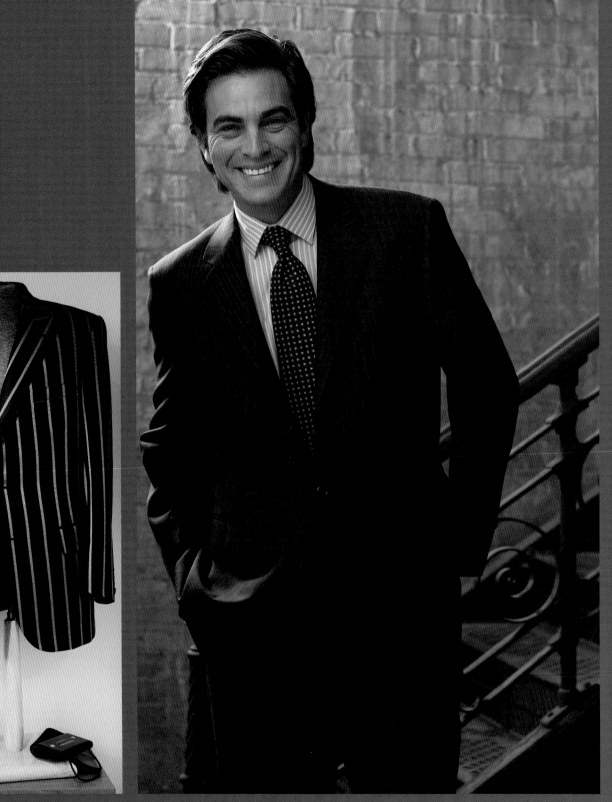

Two young men just out of business school, both graduated with honors.

Both earned masters. Both are looking for executive-level careers, and both have been granted an interview with the same Fortune 500 Company.

This is the opportunity of which they've both dreamed. This would be the payoff for those six long years of academic sweat.

There's only one job open. Someone gets the prize; someone goes home empty-handed.

If you were a gambling man, you'd probably put your money on the candidate with the longest resume.

Hot tip: Don't bet on it.

The one who ends up with the company parking space didn't look as good on paper. He looked great in person.

He walked in looking like he already had the job.

Shoes shined professionally. Tailored dark suit with a crisp white shirt and conservatively colorful tie. Solid eye contact during the initial firm handshake. He even stood to hold the door for the interviewer's personal assistant to enter the office first.

Nice touch.

Like it or not, the impression a man makes in first-time situations has less to do with what he has accomplished than how he dresses, how he carries himself, how he behaves towards others.

Rail against the superficiality of snap judgment all you want. It's human nature. It's all part of being a member of the kingdom/phylum/class/order/family/genus/species of animal. We rely first on our senses to determine whether other creatures are approachable. How others look, smell, sound, and behave give us important clues. Don't ignore them.

That's why when you walk in a door, others decide in mere seconds if they want to know more about you. Or not.

Supposing you've done your homework and they're interested, congratulations. Your work is just beginning. Now is the time to prove them right. Show them their first impression was spot on. Demonstrate with follow-up and follow-through, with knowing what to do next, and how to do it. Keep them charmed every day thereafter.

Don't worry. It's all here in this book. When the time comes to seal the deal, to host the business lunch to close the deal, and to spend the evening with the chairman of the board celebrating the deal, you'll know exactly what to do. You'll know what to wear, which fork to use, where and when to tip, and all those added touches that etch good impressions.

In other words, you'll know how to conduct yourself in the realm of success.

It's all about professionalism. Projecting an image that speaks to your level of confidence and inspires it in others. That's the quality we look for in everyone else, from the person who serves us lunch to the one who advises us on life's biggest decisions. Why would we expect anything less from ourselves?

Put simply, learning to package yourself appropriately shines the right light on your best self and, in the process, makes others feel comfortable in your company. There's nothing inauthentic about either. Nor is there anything difficult. Amazing how many guys get it wrong.

Aren't you glad?

Here's where choice comes in. You can choose to ignore the basics of personal presentation herein and continue to wonder why the track isn't as fast as you envisioned. Or, you can mind a few details and enjoy the results.

Bottom line? Business, social, romance: clothes, grooming, courtesy, confidence, professionalism count.

This book is about making sure they count in your favor.

It means getting your foot in some extremely important doors.

Specifically, doors that open.

Enjoy.

BUSIN
BUS
BU

A Tom James wardrobe

The Young Executive Wardrobe
The Executive's Wardrobe
Business Casual

We've all seen them. Those huge, walk-in, mahogany-lined, compartmentalized closets with brass rods. Beautiful custom-tailored suits hanging in a perfect row. A wardrobe of dress shirts. A coordinated selection of blazers, sports coats, and trousers. A line of shoes, starting with dark leather lace-ups, ending with athletic shoes. Casual and sports clothing folded and tucked neatly into the flush, built-in drawers. Ditto for accessories. Cashmere robe draped over a hook.

Chances are this is not your closet. Not yet, anyway.

But this is the closet to which we aspire. Don't despair if your current storage is nothing more than one rod, a clumsy top shelf, and a floor full of heaven-knows-what. What's hanging there is our current concern. It should be yours, too.

There's hope. As with many things in life, one step at a time.

We start here with the staple of an aspiring professional's wardrobe: the suit. If you can afford only one at the moment, that's OK. Make sure it's the right one. We'll help. Then we'll begin building a basic business wardrobe.

Beyond that, we'll explore the elements of the executive closet, the kind pictured here. We'll look at custom tailoring, exquisite fabrics, refined details, and the kind of style that becomes a successful man's signature.

This is where the fun starts.

You

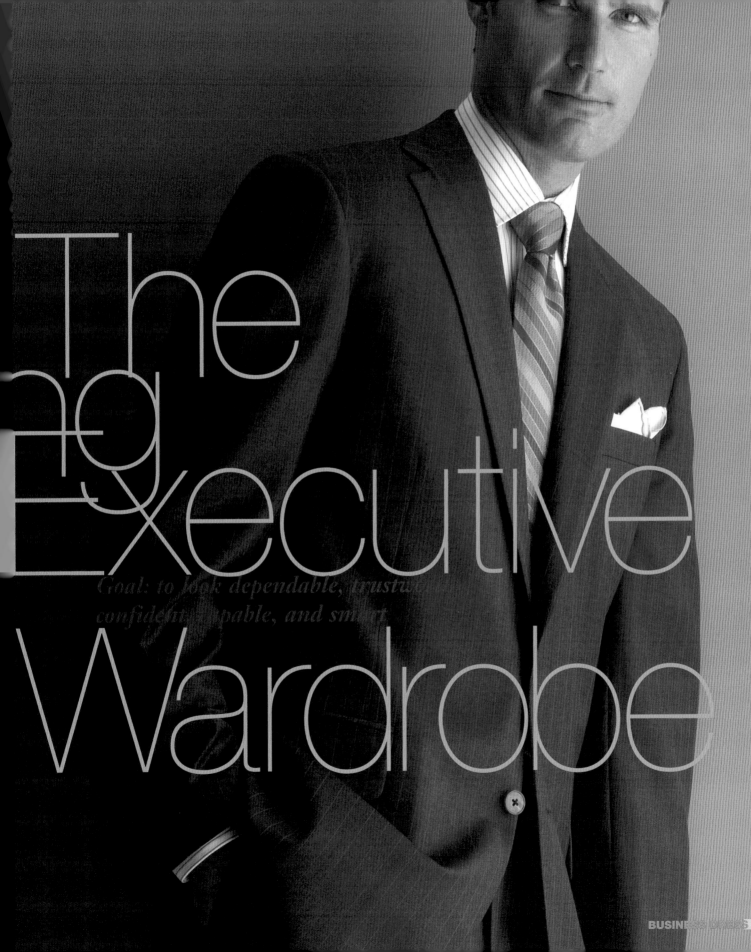

The Executive Wardrobe

Goal: to look dependable, trustworthy, confident, capable, and smart

THE GOOD SUIT

Fresh out of academia, every man needs a suit. It is required for many occasions, among them meetings with prospective employers, bankers, investors, and others in whom you wish to inspire trust. You may think your college navy blazer exudes polish, but you would be mistaken. The look is not appropriate for interviews and the executive-level positions to follow. Unless you are applying to run a dorm.

As always, consulting a professional is the best way to come out looking like one. That means shopping with an expert who knows fine menswear. We don't mean your girlfriend.

We mean you should buy from someone who specializes in fine menswear, either at an upscale department store (good), a shop devoted to men's clothing (better), or from someone who does wardrobe planning and custom tailoring for executives (best). At this level of retail, you should get sound advice and the assurance of knowledgeable alterations should you need them. This is what Tom James Company does.

Keep in mind that the motivation behind this first suit and the next few to follow is not to look fashionable and hip. You aren't dressing to get dates here.

You are dressing to get hired. Then promoted. Which, come to think of it, will probably get you dates.

The looks we suggest are timeless, conservative, and always in good taste. There are millions of other professional clothing choices out there, some of them acceptable. But for now, we are less concerned with style than with foolproof. Save those expressions of your unique self for the more established phase of your life.

Right now, your primary goal is to look dependable, trustworthy, and confident. You want the person sitting across the desk or lunch table from you to feel comfortable and find you credible. While much of the impression is up to you personally, the way you package yourself also communicates these qualities—or doesn't.

Remember, this is your one and only suit. For the moment, anyway. We are certain it is the first in what will be a fine wardrobe. The kind of wardrobe housed in a mahogany closet, if you wish.

REAL LIFE 101
PLAN AHEAD

Too many men assume the to-do list should read 1) Line up interview. 2) Buy interview clothing.

The problem with this logic is that quality fit usually requires alterations. Finding the right pair of shoes in the right size may require several stops. New shirts will have to be laundered before being worn to release packaging folds. Clothing

should look fresh, but never brand-new. The idea is to appear comfortable and seasoned in your executive look.

The bottom line: You can't shop at 10:00 a.m. Monday for a 1:00 p.m. Monday interview. You may not be able to shop at 10:00 a.m. Monday for a 1:00 p.m. Wednesday interview.

Pulling it all together for the way you want to look requires time and care. Shop at least a week before you will actually need the clothing, longer if it's custom made.

Let this be a lesson in the value of advance planning. Throughout life, it will serve you well.

THE YOUNG EXECUTIVE WARDROBE

QUALITY

If you can only afford one suit at the moment, make it the best suit you can afford. Many important first impressions are riding on it. This is one of those times when testing the limits of your credit card is not only acceptable, it's advisable. **An investment in your wardrobe is an investment in your future—a wise investment. How people see you today is how they remember you tomorrow.**

Quality not only makes a good impression; it makes good sense. The better the quality, the better the suit will wear and last. If you own only one, it's going to need all the help it can get.

How do you determine quality? Price is one indicator, but not the only indicator. In this case, the most expensive suit may not be the right choice. What you want is a conservative, attractive suit that fits and doesn't look cheap. **You want durability, not luxury.** Here are the things to look for:

- The suit should be lined and constructed. Lining is the slick fabric that helps you slip into the jacket without friction. It should be silk or silk-like rayon and smoothly attached. Poorly sewn lining causes puckers in the suit. The construction forms the suit's skeleton. You can't see this canvas-like construction fabric, but you should be able to feel its stiffness around the shoulders and chest. Think of it as the hidden frame inside a convertible top that gives lasting shape. It's important. On the better suits, this canvas interlining is stitched, not glued.

- Look at all the outside seams. There should be no uneven lines or puckering. Pay special attention to the armholes front and back, where puckering is most apt to occur.

- Turn sideways to the mirror and inspect the neckline. The collar should lie perfectly flat against the neck and shoulders, with no gap. Lift your arms and put them back down. The jacket should return to this flat position.

- Buttons should be imitation horn (as in water buffalo). Avoid cheap plastic, which breaks and/or deteriorates with cleaning. Plastic buttons are solid and will match exactly. Horn will be less even in color with visible veins running through them.

- Buttonholes should be neatly stitched with no straggly threads. Test them by buttoning and unbuttoning repeatedly as you try on the suit. Make sure no threads spring free. If it has imitation or sham buttonholes on cuffs, they, too, should be flawless.

- Pockets should be real and usable, not just bogus slits or flaps. But keep your hands and a preponderance of stuff out of them. Weight and pulling ruin a jacket's shape.

SHOULDERS ARE
SEWN BY HAND

THE ARMHOLE IS
SEWN BY HAND

COAT LININGS
ARE MADE
WITH VERTICAL
CHEST PLEATS

100% CUPRO
BEMBERG BODY
LINING SLIGHTLY
CONTRASTING
TO FABRIC

DOUBLE LAYERED
FUNCTIONAL ARM
SHIELDS SEWN
BY HAND

TRUE PASSPORT
POCKET WITH A
FLAP TO BUTTON

SEPARATE PEN
AND PENCIL
POCKET INSIDE
LEFT COAT FRONT

GLASSES CASE
POCKET LINED
WITH CHAMOIS

BUSINESS CARD
POCKET INSIDE
LEFT COAT LINING

Why wool? Many reasons.
It resists wear and tear, soil,
and wrinkles. It conforms
smoothly to the body's contours.

Try this: Before selecting and
trying on a wool suit, crush the
fabric gently in your hand.
A good wool should bounce back
to its original shape.

FABRIC

Another good indicator of quality is the look and feel of the fabric. Rule No. 1: Your starter suit (and most thereafter) should be 100 percent wool.

Why wool? Many reasons. It resists wear and tear, soil, and wrinkles. It is most comfortable because it both insulates against cold and wicks away perspiration—properties that help regulate the body's natural temperature. It conforms smoothly to the body's contours and absorbs up to one-third its weight in moisture before feeling wet to the touch. Perhaps most of all for your purposes, wool outlasts other fabrics.

Wool goes by many names—merino, worsted, tropical, gabardine, flannel, Super 100, etc. Don't let that throw you. What you want here is a midweight wool to serve year-round. Generally speaking, the fabric will be flat, not thick or coarse to the touch.

Of course, keep in mind what works year-round in Boston differs dramatically from what works year-round in Miami.

At this point, it's best to stay away from "wool blends." Some of them are perfectly acceptable, desirable even. But some have heavy doses of synthetics you don't want. Selecting this first suit is like ordering a strange dish in a foreign country. You can't be sure what's in it. With 100 percent wool, you're sure.

That said, you should also understand that not all 100 percent wool suits are created equally. The price tags will tell you that. What separates the several-hundred-dollar wool suit from those costing thousands begins with the quality of the fibers and how those fibers are milled and woven.

A short lesson: When sheep are sheared, wool fleeces are separated into classes, or "matchings," a term derived from the fact that fiber varies in length, diameter, and overall condition from one part of the sheep to another. The finer the hair, the better the quality. The best typically comes from the protected underside. Fibers then go to be processed at a mill and are thereafter woven into fabric.

While we won't go into the intricacies of the milling and weaving processes, one term you should know is "two-ply wool." This indicates two yarns have been twisted together, a good thing because it gives fabric strength to last.

You may not yet be ready for the luxurious underbelly fibers processed in the finest mills, but you still want the best quality you can afford. Try this: Before selecting and trying on a wool suit, crush the fabric gently in your hand. A good wool should bounce back to its original shape (or reasonable facsimile thereof). If it doesn't, just think how you'll look getting off the L.A.-to-New York flight. It's a signal to move on to a better quality fabric.

The fabric should be rich in color and not reflect the light. Through its Holland & Sherry mill in Tome, Chile, Tom James Company mills the finest wool fabrics in the world, super 120s, 140s, 160s, and 180s.

COLOR

Solid navy or charcoal gray is the best choice for your only suit. These colors will take you everywhere from interviews to boardrooms, business lunches to cocktail receptions, weddings to funerals.

Avoid patterns like bold pinstripes for this one suit. Patterns may be classic, but they're not as flexible as solids and are more tiring. You'll have plenty of time and money for pattern later.

Of the two colors, we lean toward charcoal gray. Charcoal is the confidence color. It's subdued and elegant and makes a young man look experienced. Gray makes good first impressions because it's less common, less severe, more upscale. You won't look like the last guy who came in or the one before him or the one before him. They all wore navy suits.

If you're fortunate enough to have both, wear charcoal for the first interview and the navy suit for follow-up. Navy is the power color. Wear it when it's time to negotiate.

Do not confuse charcoal gray with black. Although the black business suit has gained acceptance in contemporary fashion and is widely seen abroad, it is not mainstream among American executives in all regions of the country. It shouldn't be your first or second suit. Maybe your eighth or ninth.

CUT

Once upon a time, there were three distinct cuts of suit. These were American, British, and Italian. But globalization has made the world a much smaller place. That applies to men's suits, too, where so much cross-pollination has blurred conventional categories. What once was distinctively Italian, for example, can now be found among the most conservative American labels.

If you want to talk the talk, the new breeds are known as traditional, updated traditional, and fashion. But walking the walk is more important for your first suit. For now, all you need to know is this: two-button or three-button single-breasted, single-vent jacket with natural shoulder and pleated or plain-front trousers with cuffs. This suit is elegant, classic, and timeless.

It's also updated traditional, if you must know.

THE THREE-PIECE SUIT

You may be puzzled by the omission of the three-piece suit in this lineup, since it is often considered the most classic of gentlemanly suits.

Despite its genteel roots, the three-piece has become more a fashion statement than a wardrobe staple and is thus subject to ebb and flow of popularity. Yet it remains an elegant alternative in an extended wardrobe. It affords two distinct advantages: an added layer for colder climates and a more polished look for those who dispense with their suit jackets in an office.

Still, it is not the choice for those of you building a young wardrobe. It's more expensive than two pieces and appears a tad pretentious or overdressed for a young man. You're not ready for the pocket watch chain or, perish the thought, a dangle for your Phi Beta Kappa key. Stick with two pieces.

IT MATTERS

S

Are there do's and don'ts for cut depending on physical build? Yes and no. There are few absolutes, but several wise suggestions. And remember there is no substitute for great fit.

- Tall men can wear most anything, graced as they are. But they should avoid bold pinstripes, as these emphasize a vertical line. Weighty fabrics such as tweeds are good, as are Glen plaids and windowpane checks. Cuffs on pants and pocket flaps are recommended. Tall men wear double-breasted and longer, more contemporary cuts well, if they so choose.

- Short men should think vertical. Keep details to a minimum. Avoid wide lapels, baggy pants, and cuffs. The idea is for the eye to travel top to bottom with little interruption. Pass on long jackets and double-breasted. Shorter jackets elongate legs. Stick with single-breasted, two-button jackets, which reveal more shirt and tie. Choose pinstripes and medium to dark solids. No bold plaids or checks.

- Heavyset guys (you know who you are) can still look nice while exercising and eating right to lose that excess baggage. Right? Don't fool yourself into thinking less suit translates visually into less you. *Au contraire.* Your suit must fit generously and impeccably, not tugging at any seam. Stick with medium to dark colors. Avoid patterns and light colors like they were a heaping of mashed potatoes. Muted stripes, hairline stripe, nails' head, and tic weave are the best patterns. Choose single-breasted two-button, crisp lapel, and strong shoulder. In this case, drawing the eye upward is a good thing.

TO BUTTON OR NOT TO BUTTON, THAT IS THE QUESTION

This isn't hard:
- Never button the bottom button on your suit jacket.
- Always button the one above it.
- If there are three, buttoning the top is optional. But you neither want to conceal the long line of your tie, nor look uptight. Sometimes buttoning the top can affect both.

The mark of a custom-tailored, expensive suit—one of them, anyway—is sleeve cuffs that actually button. Many suits have imitation or sham holes, but only the full custom suit can be made with "surgeon sleeves" that open fully.

Buttons on cuffs originated centuries ago when men weren't at liberty to remove their coats, but had to perform tasks—like surgery, for example—that might soil their suit sleeves. Unbuttoning allowed the sleeves to be pushed up.

We no longer have such needs, thank heavens, but the extra handwork of functional buttonholes speaks to a suit's quality. Some men relish those details.

OFF THE CUFF

Suit trousers sit at the waist, just at the navel— not below it like jeans.

KILLER
ANKLES RANKLE

When having suit pants hemmed, make sure you are wearing the dress shoes you intend to wear with the suit. The hem should be one and three-quarters to two inches up from the floor at the heel of the shoe. This will cause trousers to "break," or pool slightly, over the top of the shoe. This is fine. It looks elegant. The point is to cover the entire sock as you stand and allow only a modicum of sock to show when walking.

Some men don't get this and subsequently roam the earth with socks and shoes gleefully exposed. This is not-so-affectionately known as "high water" trousers and makes the wearer look pedestrian. Especially when he sits down, revealing his bare shins and beyond, assuming he hasn't gotten the memo for over-the-calf hose.

This isn't elementary school anymore. You're not going to trip over your pants at recess. Make sure they are long enough. It's a welcome sign of maturity.

{ Tip: Pants should have 1¹/₂- to 1³/₄-inch cuffs, depending on the wearer's height. }

KILLER
VENTING

If you have ever had the misfortune of wearing a hospital gown, you understand the concept of rear-vented clothing and the indignity therein.

Picture that same effect in a suit. Although there is one notable difference, viewing a man's panted posterior through a split jacket vent is still off-putting and the mark of inferior fit.

When buying a suit, look at the rear in a mirror. Do vent flaps overlap for full closure? Do they match the line of the hem when closed? Button the jacket. The vent(s) should remain closed. Only when you put your hand in your pants pocket should it part slightly.

TAKING CARE OF BUSINESS (SUITS)

Proper care is essential to maintain this precious first suit and every one thereafter. Take note:

• Rule No. 1: Hang it up. As soon as you get home. Never use a wire hanger. Use a wide solid wood hanger curved like shoulders. Trousers should hang with inner seams lined up and cuffs together, either folded over a hanger with a wooden dowel, or straight and held by the cuff on a trouser hanger. The latter is good for relaxing wrinkles, but can misshape cuffs if left hanging too long. Since this is your only suit at the moment, not much chance of that.

• If a suit gets damp, allow it to breathe and dry. Don't put it in the closet. Instead, hang it on a proper wooden hanger over the back of an open door for a few hours or overnight.

• When the wrinkled from too much everyday wear or traveling, hang it in a closed bathroom and turn the shower on hot. Steam works wonders. Just be careful not to let the suit get near the shower. Wet is not what you want.

DEAL KILLER
WHEN NOT TO SHINE

There eventually comes a point in the relationship when man must part with his beloved dark suit and select another. This point is often signaled by a distinct shine on the fabric resulting from too much wear, cleaning, and/or pressing. One solution is to purchase a second pair of trousers with each suit.

• View dry cleaning like the dentist. It's something you must do, but as infrequently as possible. The chemicals and heat are very hard on a suit's fabric and structure. It will wear much longer if you avoid the cleaners until it's absolutely necessary. Shoot for every six months, three at worst. Purchase a spot cleaner and use it if necessary. It will save both your money and your suit. If you get caught in a downpour or frequent humid climates, having the suit pressed occasionally by professionals revives it without cleaning. For best results, never wear a garment directly from the dry cleaners. Always remove and discard the plastic dry cleaner bags. Allow it to dry twenty-four hours in your closet.

• Remove your suit coat before sitting down for extended periods on planes and trains and in cars. If possible, hang it up; if not, gently fold it in half vertically along the back center seam (lapels and lining will be facing out). Then lay it down on a seat or overhead bin as flatly as possible. Sitting in a suit jacket causes excessive wrinkling.

• Keep a lint roller or good lint brush at home, at the office, and in the car. Better still: Use it. Especially those of you living with blondes, referring, of course, to golden retrievers. Sticky tape (Scotch, packing, duct) will do in a pinch.

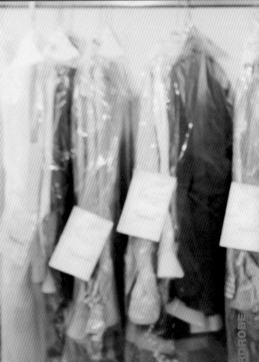

BUILDING YOUR
TOM JAMES
WARDROBE

How many suits a man ultimately owns depends on three D's: desire, dollars, and duties.

Some occupations may require only a couple of suits for occasional wear. He may get by with two or three suits total.

In most professional occupations, however, the suit is a four- to five-day-per-week necessity. For this man, the selection can be as broad as his sensibilities and wallet allow. Obviously, he needs a bigger suit wardrobe. We suggest he owns a minimum of five.

The following is a guideline of how to build that wardrobe. It focuses on the first five suits needed for a professional's wardrobe.

From there, the sky is the limit.

The first five suits

We've talked about the first suit in which a young professional should invest: a charcoal or navy in super 100s. . . the best you can afford. . . and conservatively cut. Much of what you've learned about this first suit applies to the next four.

Building the Young Wa

As soon as possible, it is wise to also acquire a winter wardrobe of five suits using the same guideline.

After the first suit, the lineup should look something like this:

2nd suit: If your first suit was **charcoal**, the second should be **solid navy**—and vice versa.

3rd suit: **A medium to dark gray stripe** fabric. The difference between pinstripe and chalk stripe goes beyond one word or two. Pinstripe is a very fine, thin line spaced anywhere from one-sixteenth inch to one and one-half inches. Chalk stripe is thicker and wider. Neither, in case you were wondering, should resemble cheesy gangster attire.

In this overscheduled world, it's tempting to put off the non-urgent until it's, well, urgent. While we are all for being in the moment, a certain amount of looking ahead is advised where wardrobing is concerned.

This is especially true of seasonal wardrobes. By considering what's in "storage" a few weeks before the season arrives, you can be ready for the first temperature shift. Does anything need dry cleaning? ("No" is the correct answer, since suits should be cleaned before hanging them back for the season to discourage moths and stains setting in.) Are there buttons missing or other alterations needed? Does anything smell like moth balls? (Again, the correct answer is "no," since you've wisely discovered cedar and lavender as fragrant alternatives.)

Answer "yes" to any of the above and the first warm spring day could find you in a sweat.

Besides, if you need to update or upgrade—it's time to replace an older suit or the raincoat is looking sad—it's better to shop early in the season. Later on, selection may suffer.

Executive wardrobe

PROFESSIONAL ADVICE: IT'S NOT WHAT YOU HAVE BUT HOW YOU USE IT

In the early stages of wardrobe building, you may own only a few ties. That's OK if you maximize what you have. Do this by draping ties over each coat instead of hanging them on a hook or tie rack. After you wear one, flip it over and hang it on the suit. The next day, you'll know to select another. Keep reversing each tie after you wear it once until you've worn them all. Then start back with the first. This forced rotation stretches your wardrobe. It's also a good refresher for the man with an endless selection of ties who tends to wear the same favorites constantly.

4th suit: A **navy pinstripe** (see note on 3rd suit).

5th suit: A **blue-gray** in a solid, nail's head, or tic weave fabric. Nail's head and tic weave are both fabrics woven with a microscopic pattern overall. The effect is solid, but the fabric has an ever-so-slight texture.

These five suits afford many different looks, all of which fall within the realm of professional good taste. The following sections on shirts and ties will demonstrate how these five suits can be expanded into a whole host of ensembles. Don't worry; you won't need a number system to remember what goes with what. These suits and the recommended shirt and tie wardrobes outlined next represent basic, foolproof combinations for polished looks. In simpler terms, it all mixes and matches. Mistakes will be almost impossible.

THE POWER OF COLOR

Color has a language all its own, even the subtle shades found in fine business suits. It behooves you to speak a little of it.

- Dark gray, as we have said, is a confidence color. It gets you noticed without intimidating others. It's good for first interviews, meetings with clients, and most anything else you can think of.

- Navy is a more powerful color. Wear it to negotiations in which being successful trumps being liked. Meetings with bankers come to mind.

- Black is a severe color. It conveys confidence and power, but with an edge. For some more traditional types, the black suit still denotes funereal, artsy, or brutish in a business setting. That's why you should be careful where you wear it and with whom. Of course, it's the color for formal attire.

- Brown and olive are warm and masculine. They do not have the presence or authority of a navy or gray suit, but that can be a good thing, as President Ronald Reagan often demonstrated. Browns project a friendly image and are great for rapport-building. Wear them to staff meetings or anytime you want to be non-confrontational. They're perfect for the dominant man who needs to come across as approachable.

- Tan is a neutral color. People tend to remember a tan suit, which is often thought of as a rich man's color because he can afford the dry cleaning bill. Provided the fabric is fine and shirt and tie colors are conservatively balanced, tan's neutrality can be to summer what charcoal and navy are to winter—ultimately flexible and universally acceptable.

Shirts

Assuming the first suit is a handsome charcoal gray and the second is navy, we turn our focus to shirts. This is how you transform that suit into a wardrobe.

Even if you are just starting your career, it is wise to acquire your first five suits as quickly as possible, so that you can avoid wearing any suit more than once each week.

When building a classic wardrobe, remember that fashion changes very slowly, so anything you buy today may be just as appropriate five years from now as well. Many men find joy and pleasure in working with their Tom James professional to build their wardrobes. Often those who can afford it build their wardrobes to be extensive enough to never wear the same combination (suit, shirt, and tie) twice in the same month.

Regardless of where you live, except in the tropics, you will be better served to have a separate wardrobe for summer and for winter.

Shirts are important. The color, fit, and fabric of your shirts need to be right, as do the ties that go with them.

{ Tip: A shirt collar should show above the jacket collar at least one-half inch. }

You probably guessed your first important shirt would be white. Congratulations. You're showing promise.

But before you break out the cigars, there are a few details about getting the right white shirt that you may not know. Yet.

Fabric

Dress shirts should be 100 percent cotton. Buying a wash-and-wear blend may be tempting for the sake of budget and easy care, but it doesn't have the polish of pure cotton. Stick with the real thing and, unless you're massively talented with an iron, send your shirts to the laundry. Professionally laundered shirts resist wrinkles better over the course of a day. Have them returned on hangers unless you need to pack them in a bag, in which case have them folded. Better still, invest in a suit bag that carries shirts on hangers.

Like wools, there is an entire vocabulary of cottons. Some of the best designations for dress shirts are Pima, Egyptian, and Sea Island. These have a satin-like texture and feel divine next to the skin. On the next tier are poplin and broadcloth, followed by oxford cloth. The more coarse the texture, the less fine the cotton.

STIFFED AGAIN

How much to starch a shirt is a matter of personal preference and comfort. You want it somewhere between limp and "stands upright by itself." Each laundry's designation for "light," "medium," and "heavy" differs, so experiment. Even if you request "no starch," collar and cuffs should still come back pristine and reinforced from being pressed while wet. That's OK.

Know that starch is hard on fabric and decreases the life of the shirt. But a starched shirt looks crisp and professional, so the trade-off in longevity is worthwhile.

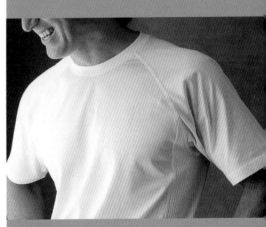

UNDERSHIRTS

If your dress shirts tend to be transparent—and many of the better cottons are—an undershirt is wise. Undershirts also absorb excessive perspiration. A plain, white, crew neck T-shirt works best. The rest may create unsightly lines that lurk beneath the dress shirt like an evil alter ego. A V neck can be an alternative, but never the tank cut.

THE YOUNG EXECUTIVE WARDROBE

Pockets

The classic dress shirt doesn't have pockets, but one left breast pocket is acceptable. Two pockets are not acceptable. That is a sport shirt.

Fit

Dress shirts come nicely folded and packaged for the most part, and you don't want to make the store personnel angry by undoing all that to try one on. Instead, know your neck size and sleeve length, measurements easily determined with a tape measure. Measure around the neck just below the Adam's apple. For comfort, choose the collar size that's one-half inch larger up to size 16^1/$_2$ and three-fourths inch to one inch over for sizes 17 and larger. The collar will not only be more comfortable, but it will also look better as your very busy day turns to evening activities.

Measure the sleeve from the beginning of the shoulder to one inch below the wrist bone.

Since the shirt he's buying is 100 percent cotton, the wise man chooses a half size beyond his measurements in collar and sleeve length. This compensates for inevitable laundry shrinkage.

If, by chance, you are fortunate enough to buy a really fine cotton dress shirt at this stage, you may be told they are already made to shrink to the correct size. Nonetheless, buy an extra half size larger. These shirts even look best after a couple of launderings.

For best results, contact your Tom James professional for measurements and to help you select shirts.

DEAL KILLER
THE SHORT-SLEEVED DRESS SHIRT

There is no place in a professional's wardrobe for a short-sleeved dress shirt. Even in the warmest climates, they will not do. They make the wearer look blue-collar. If you find yourself in an untenably warm situation, you may unbutton your cuffs and roll your long sleeves up a turn or two. But never resort to short sleeves. You are not a gym teacher from the 1950s.

DEAL KILLER
STUFFED SHIRT

The only things that should ever grace your shirt pocket are one pen and/or your reading glasses, if necessary. It's not for your Palm Pilot, cell phone, or any other weighty distraction—literally and figuratively. Those inclined to load it might as well line it with a plastic pocket protector. It's the same image. And, while you're at it, throw in a safety pin to hold the earpiece on your glasses.

Shirt collars may look pretty much alike, but there are subtle and important differences. Collars frame the face. When you are talking, your shirt collar and tie knot are the two things most people see, provided they're paying attention. It's essential that these two elements be flattering.

Collars boil down to five basic styles: regular spread, narrow/point, button-down, British spread, and tab. You might have seen other variations like rounded collars and exaggerated points, but those are for the fashion forward and, for now, that shouldn't be you.

The main thing to remember when choosing a collar is the frame should complement the picture. Again, contact your Tom James professional for best results.

- A large head or prominent jaw calls for a significant collar. A spread collar with some depth to it would be appropriate. A small collar only makes the head and jaw look more overbearing.
- A wide or round face is balanced by a medium to long collar.
- A narrow face is balanced by a spread collar.
- A long neck calls for a spread with a high collar.
- A small head and face are balanced with a slightly smaller collar.

Is there one collar that looks good on almost everyone? Yes. The safe bet is a medium spread collar with medium point. But in collars as in life, don't be eager to settle for safe when healthy exploration can lead to greater satisfaction.

Button-downs

For purposes of professional dress, button-down collars are second choice. They look somewhat collegiate, as was their Ivy League origin, and therefore less polished than a straight collar. They can also behave badly when paired with an incompatible tie and/or expansive neck. The combination causes the strained collar to bell out on either side in front like certain European nuns' hats. To say this ruins a look ranks under "gross understatement."

Some collars come with buttons on the underneath side to discreetly anchor the points. These are fine, as long as the tailoring is quality and the points don't ultimately curve up beyond the button.

If you are overly fond of button-down collars, despair not. Button-downs are perfectly acceptable for dress-down business (see Business Casual in this chapter) in quality solids or quiet patterns. They are best paired with blazers and sport coats, because they are less dressy than other collars.

KILLER DEAL
NOT SHARP

Collar pins never go on buttoned-down collars. Never. For all the good it will do your professional image, you might as well stick it through your earlobe as in your buttoned-down collar.

STUDY IN CONTRASTS

A white collar on a colored shirt—say a nice soft blue shade, for example—is a classic look that denotes elegance. There is nothing wrong with this except it is not mainstream and, therefore, not the safest choice for the young executive trying to make good initial impressions.

Collar pins

Yes, they look very elegant—and these days, overdressed on a young man. Like the tie tack, bracelet, and almost all other male jewelry, the collar pin adds unnecessary flash. It looks like you're trying too hard.

Tab collars

Tab collars are straight collars with a little connecting piece of fabric that snaps beneath the tie to hold the collar in place. Tab collars are not as popular today but are enjoyed and worn by men who love custom shirts.

Fit

The secret of an attractive shirt collar is that it's large enough to be worn comfortably all day while buttoned. It should never exert pressure. That's why the collar should always be one-half inch to three-quarters of an inch away. The heavier the man, the more room the collar should have.

{ Tip: Collar stays—those little removable reinforcements that slip down inside collar points—are your friend. They're not something the manufacturer put there for you to throw away. They keep your tips from curling up and the collar looking clean and neat. Take them out before the shirt goes to the laundry each time for safekeeping and put them back in when you wear it. In a pinch, a paper clip might work. }

The collar of a dress shirt should fit closely, but you should be able to insert a finger behind the top button or any other portion of the collar when it's fastened. Any more room signifies it is too big. Any less and you can't swallow.

Conversely, beware the pinch fit. That's when your skin folds over the top. It makes everyone uncomfortable, wearer and viewer alike. Since our neck size expands when we sit, it's best not to make a size decision while standing.

CUFFS

Like collars, cuffs come in a variety of shapes and details. But unlike collars, your choice need not be predicated on any particular physical feature.

For the young man's purposes, there are two choices: a regular button cuff, sometimes called a "barrel" cuff, and French cuffs that require cuff links. If you choose the latter, make sure you know what you're doing. That means only the most discreet, tasteful cuff links. *You* are supposed to be the conversation piece, not your accessories.

{ Tip: The shirt cuff should show approximately one-quarter to one-half inch below the suit jacket sleeve. }

Button-down collars require button cuffs, but dress collars can be paired with either button or French cuffs, or as the English prefer to call them, double cuffs. Most dress shirts in England are double cuff. These cuffs are generally regarded as dressier than button cuffs, underscored by their appearance as the standard in all formalwear. This reputation makes them seem overdressed when worn with a sports jacket.

Beyond this, all you need to know is cuffs should fall about one inch below your wrist bone and close tightly enough to stay there.

Yokes

The yoke is the upper back part of the shirt. The finest handmade shirts feature a split yoke, indicated by a vertical seam between the shoulders that allows each shoulder to be fitted individually. Most will be flat across the back with some subtle pleating to help arms and shoulders move. The thing to ensure here is that your shirts aren't too tight across the yoke. Cross your arms in front to make sure you have ample movement. For the neatest appearance, the yoke and sleeve seam should not drop below the shoulder, but should line up where your arm joins the shoulder.

MONOGRAMS

Monograms were originally instituted so men would get their property back from the laundry. They have evolved into a matter of taste and extra adornment. Some consider them good taste; others consider them too flashy. Therefore, assuming you are just starting your journey to professional status, it's best to leave such designation off. You do not want to appear pretentious and, to some, monogramming does.

If and when the time comes for displaying your initials on your shirts, several rules apply. One, the monogram should be simple, discreet, and *tiny*, smaller than three-eights of an inch. As if you don't really care that anyone sees it.

As for positioning, the purveyors of all things classic favor four inches to the left of the shirt's center button line or at the waist. If there is a pocket, it centers that pocket or falls below it. The thread color can be a dark contrast or a pale shade one step below the shirt's hue. Monogrammed cuffs are not

The Shirt Ward

Now that you understand the basics of a good dress shirt, you are ready to buy twelve. Why twelve? This number allows you to put five in the laundry each week and have seven to wear. Remember, one clean shirt should remain at your office at all times in case the waiter spills soup on you during lunch. **You can never afford to be unprepared.**

Note there is no dark-colored dress shirt. It is not traditionally business; it is fashion. Add the serious classic shirts first; then you can branch out.

In our palette of pales, we have also left off yellow, pink, green, and purple. Although some of these can be added in your second dozen shirts, none is recommended for an important day in a young professional's career.

When expanding the shirt wardrobe, you want to think about variety to give your basic dark suits life and legs. Consider:

- three white solids
- one white solid with French cuffs
- four blue solids
- one navy stripe
- one red stripe
- one burgundy stripe
- one black or gray small pattern (stripe or small check)

robe

SLEEVE

Ties

Ties are important for the same reasons shirts are, if not more so. They are what everyone sees if you remove your coat at the office, and, like the shirt collar, they enhance the face. The vertical tie not only covers the shirt buttons; it makes you appear taller, neater, and slimmer.

Properly selected and worn, a tie can make or break a man's image. Ties reflect a man's taste and individuality, or lack thereof. In short, ties are the one thing most likely to get you noticed, for better or worse.

Don't assume any old tie will do. You can't step out in your fine new charcoal suit, crisp white shirt, and a tie you've had since high school. Someone *will* notice.

As endless as the selection of ties is, the basics are few. The tie should always be silk, wool, or knit.

The tie should feel supple to the touch, but not limp or soft. It should have tangible body. All quality ties have a wool inner construction that keeps the shape intact. You can feel this.

The reason body and inner structure are important is they help the tie hold its knot and bounce back into shape after wearing. The finished knot should be taut and have a lasting dimple. Limp ties can't hold their dimple.

Last, but not least, remember the tie is your friend. It is the least expensive way to refresh and expand your fledgling wardrobe. Always purchase at least four ties with each suit or sports coat. Each tie is a small investment that will expand your small wardrobe.

Width

What's acceptable in tie width waxes and wanes with fashion. You should be less concerned with current fad than with what works best with your suit. The tie should be in proportion to the jacket's lapels, which in turn should be in proportion to the jacket's shoulder. In the case of your starter suit, all of these widths should be moderate.

Another point to keep in mind when selecting a tie is the type of shirt collar you favor. A spread collar calls for a substantial knot, and a narrow collar requires a small knot. The width of the tie determines that, as does the knot itself. The four-in-hand knot is good for medium to narrow spread collars, and the double or half-windsor is good for wide spread collars.

Still feeling insecure? A safe width is three and one-half inches.

Here are some suggestions to help you begin to navigate the vast waters of tie patterns and color.

- Woven silk ties look richer than printed silk.
- The classic rep tie with its even diagonal stripe is always appropriate.
- Solid ties lack imagination unless worn as a complement to bold stripes or other patterned shirts that need softening.
- Some patterns and colors are seasonal. Maroons and golds are fall/winter colors, while lighter blues and greens are more spring/summer.
- Red is a power color in ties. It creates a line pointing to the mouth that shouts "pay attention." Presidential candidates favor red ties, especially in televised debates. But bright red can also be overbearing, especially for job interviews and sensitive negotiations.
- Although polka dot ties are considered classic, they're not as safe as stripe, club, or small neats (little repetitive patterns woven or printed). Small polka dots are OK but large ones have an unfortunate history with gangsters and clowns.
- In general, ties that combine pale colors look bland and insignificant. So does their wearer. Conversely, too much bright color can be the equivalent of shouting. Land somewhere in between until you are established in your profession.
- Bright color is OK, as long as it is tempered with softer shades.
- Since the selection of patterns and colors can be overwhelming, consider seeking professional help from your Tom James clothier.

DEAL KILLER
FAMILY TIES

Chances are you may have been or will be the recipient of a gift tie. This is something someone related to you gives you because he or she can't think of anything else. Such neckwear, however well-intended, often signals trouble.

In case you find yourself so gifted, a few things to note: Any tie that's apt to elicit comment beyond "nice tie" is a bad idea for work. This includes those festooned with holiday themes, sports icons, cartoon characters, logos, symbols, hidden messages, optical illusions, fish, dollar signs, or anything else that might be termed "cute."

THE FOUR-IN-HAND

{ Tip: Keep ties in shape by loosening them at the knot only (don't pull on long ends) and by positioning all seat belts under the tie, not over it. }

Like fedoras and three-piece suits, the bow tie has moved from being the mark of a well-dressed gentleman to unnecessary punctuation. A man who wears bow ties now typically does so as a trademark. It makes him stand out—as in, you won't remember his name, but you remember he wore a bow tie.

For this reason, the bow tie is best avoided unless it is black silk and the occasion is formal. Revered as they are, or at least once were, bow ties tend to impress as a tad quirky at best, goofy at worst. At this tender point in your career, neither serves you. *Wait to wear a bow tie until you have it made.*

DEAL KILLER
TIE, MEET BELT

Ties should create a continuous line from collar to pants. To do this, the point of the necktie should cover the belt buckle, but never fall more than two inches below the top of the waistband.

The largest offense here is a tie swinging short of its mark, exposing the shirt placket, buttons, and, where applicable, girth. Conversely, the overly long tie looks droopy.

Simply adjust the length of the tie by repositioning the knot. If, in an effort to lengthen the tie, the rear portion hikes up to your chest, buy a longer tie. There are such things as extra-long ties, a must for men over 6'4" in height or who wear a size 19" collar.

BEGINNING

First, a vocabulary lesson. A few common terms describe the most traditional tie patterns.

- **Neat:** Sometimes referred to as a "foulard," this tie is covered in a small pattern that repeats continuously and regularly over a solid background.
- **Polka dot:** A repeating pattern of dots on a solid background. For executive dressing, the dots should be about the size of the buttons on your cell phone. Polka dots are usually white on a navy or burgundy background.
- **Pin dot:** A small, dressy version of the polka dot, the pin dot is a tiny pattern most often done in white on a dark blue background. It is sometimes referred to as a neat, as well.
- **Stripes:** Rep stripes are the most traditional. This is an evenly spaced, diagonal stripe, usually in two contrasting colors like navy and white or navy and red. Tasteful stripe ties can add a third or fourth color, like a thin gold stripe evenly interspersed with wider red, blue, and green stripes, for example. But, in general, stripes should be an even, repeating, all-over pattern, not an accent on an otherwise solid tie.
- **Club:** This pattern derives its name from a time when club members wore ties printed with their organization's emblem. Think "prep school." Today's club tie sports a regularly repeating pattern on a solid background that is more widely spaced than a neat. Holiday ties often fall into this category, with little candy canes or some such sprinkled across them. In general, the club tie is considered more casual. It's better for weekends with sports coats or blazers.
- **Paisley:** This pattern takes its inspiration from beautiful wool shawls made in Paisley, Scotland. The intricate, swirling design looks like something you may have seen under a microscope in biology class. Classic as they may be, paisley ties must be chosen carefully. They are considered conservative, but some can also be very bold. The key is taste, not pattern.

Starting a collection

Assuming you have purchased a handsome charcoal gray or navy suit and the recommended lineup of shirts, the following ties will help turn these into a flexible wardrobe. Note that we have given several choices. That's to save you from running all over town looking for that one specific tie. Any purveyor of fine menswear should stock some acceptable variation.

- Red or burgundy neat or dot
- Red, burgundy, navy, or black stripe
- Yellow neat or yellow and navy stripe
- Burgundy ground pattern

A TIE
WARDROBE

THE YOUNG EXECUTIVE WARDROBE

POCKET SQUARES

Pocket squares are another casualty of less formal times. Some men continue the tradition with a white linen handkerchief tucked discreetly in the business suit breast pocket. Others add a colorful silk square with a navy blazer or other sports coat, which can add a touch of color if you're not wearing a tie.

If you feel incomplete without a pocket square, a white linen or cotton handkerchief is acceptable, provided it is neatly stitched (preferably hand-hemmed) and shows no more than one-half inch.

If pocket squares become part of your ensemble now or later, some things to know:

- A silk pocket square should complement the jacket, shirt, and tie, but never match the tie.

- The white handkerchief peeks out of the pocket. The silk square can be folded like a tulip or can be made to pouf.

- Learn to fold properly. Patterned silk should look relaxed, with a purposed casualness, but solid white should show neat, rigid points and look more formal.

- The pocket handkerchief is just for show, not to be used.

Shoes

Say all you want about the importance of the suit, the shirt, the tie. The single most scrutinized feature of a man's appearance is his shoes.

Go ahead. Scoff. Nothing—*nothing*—is a bigger turnoff for men or women than bad shoes.

Why is that? Maybe it's because men easily dismiss footwear. If the suit, shirt, and tie are just right, who will notice the shoes?

It's precisely this line of thinking that gets many a man in trouble. **To others, the quality and care of a man's shoes signals his inner character because they reflect his attention to all the details of his life. It has been said that if a man can't keep his shoes in first-class condition, can he be trusted to look out for his clients.**

Men's fine dress shoes are expensive. We'll continue to concentrate on the basics, followed by wardrobe building.

BACK STIFFENER

LEATHER LINING

BELLOWS TONGUE

UPPER

TOECAP

SEAT PIECE

SHANK

TOP PIECE

HEEL

MIDDLE SOLE

FEATHER

LEATHER SOLE

Simplicity is paramount when buying dress shoes, especially your first and perhaps only pair. No buckles or tassels or straps. No thick soles or heavy, blunt toes.

LACE-UP: The first pair should be classic black lace-ups. These go by several names: oxford, blucher, brogue. They may or may not have a cap-toe.

The wing tip is another classic lace-up. With its stitched leather "wing" and perforated toe, it is a touch heavier and fussier than the plain lace-up. The reason we don't recommend it as a first shoe is because it looks a little clunky for weddings and other non-business occasions.

SLIP-ON: You will see some well-dressed businessmen wearing a black slip-on instead of lace-up. This is not the collegiate Weejun-type loafer, but a slightly heavier, more polished version with understated detailing similar to the more traditional lace-up. A tasseled version is also popular, as is the brass horse bit across the top. Even though acceptable, it exposes too much sock and is not a good business look. Better to stick with lace-ups for suits until you're more sure of yourself, as they always project more authority. Leave the loafers to business casual and weekends.

BROWN SHOES: When your wallet and wardrobe expand, add a brown shoe. In fact, the brown suede cap-toe lace-up or brown wing tip can be quite elegant with a gray flannel, blue-gray or tan gabardine suit. It's a nice contrast to the sea of black shoes and a great way to expand your options. Just be careful not to wear brown shoes with a dressy dark blue suit, unless you *really* know what you're doing. The look can backfire big time.

THE SHOE

CORDOVAN: This is sometimes referred to as "oxblood." It's a dark mahogany color with just a hint of red in it that some men wear as they would black shoes. It's available in oxfords and slip-ons. Originally, cordovan was a specific kind of choice for business dress, of leather naturally that color, tanned from horses in Spain. Today, it's mostly calfskin leathers dyed that color, so not all cordovans are created equally. The wide spectrum makes it, at best, uneven—not your first or second pair.

BOOTS: Although boots can be very masculine, they don't belong in the boardroom. Not even those short boots that look like dress shoes.

We love cowboy boots, too, but they look pretentious with a business suit. Unless you live in a Western state and the business is horses, cattle, oil, or ranching.

WARDROBE

Quality

Like so many other things in life, price is not necessarily the ultimate indicator of quality dress footwear. Details and construction are. **But most of the time your investment in quality shoes will be returned in years of comfort and enjoyment.**

{ Tip: The same pair of leather shoes should never be worn two days in a row. They need time to dry out. Buy a minimum of two pairs of black lace-ups. Wear one and leave the other at home stuffed with cedar shoe trees. Keep shoes away from drying heat. Alternate the next day. Shoes will last much longer. The goal is at least five pairs of shoes for business. A gentleman should also have a good selection of casual shoes to be worn when off the clock. }

Some hints:
• Good shoes are crafted entirely of quality leather, both uppers and soles. The word "man-made" should not apply. "Handmade," yes. "Man-made," no. Even the shoe lining should be leather for longer wear and comfort. Leather breathes. Synthetics do not.
• The sole should be stitched, not glued, to the shoe. The stitches should be so tiny, tight, and even that they almost disappear.

Fit

Never go shoe shopping on Saturday morning. Go shoe shopping late in the day when feet swell naturally. This guards against the uncomfortable surprise of a shoe that's too narrow or ill-fitting. Try on both shoes. Feet differ. Even your own.

Wear dress socks to try on shoes. Those would be the thin to medium-thin solid black variety better known as "men's hosiery." Trying on dress shoes wearing athletic socks never works. If you find yourself without the right socks, ask the salesperson if there is a pair to borrow or be a big spender and buy a pair on the spot. They'll let you keep the socks, even if you don't buy shoes.

Shoes should be comfortable in the store. Toes shouldn't bunch. The back shouldn't slip up and down on your heel as you walk. Thinking a shoe is uncomfortable because it's new is a misconception. Shoes rarely "break in," as salespeople might suggest. If they hurt in the store, odds are very good they'll hurt on the sidewalk, too. In most instances, the better the quality of shoes, the more comfortable they are and remain. And vice versa.

DEAL KILLER
THE OLD SOFT SHOE

Just because you're pounding the pavement doesn't mean you can look pedestrian. It may be a sad commentary on the state of things, but wearing a pair of orthopedically sound shoes for business and dress occasions is a no-no. We're talking about those heavenly, cushy, rubber-soled lace-ups that are supposed to look like expensive oxfords but rarely do.

Unless you have no other choice (meaning you have serious medical problems), these shoes are not a good choice for interviews and other important impressions. They look like you couldn't quite graduate out of running shoes. If your feet hurt, see a podiatrist for a pair of custom insoles that fit inside your real dress shoes.

DEAL KILLER
RUNNING OUT OF LUCK

In an effort to get exercise, some men like to walk to work. While the spirit is to be commended, the potential fashion faux pas is not. Under no circumstances should athletic shoes be worn with a suit. Should you choose to walk, do so in a high quality dress shoe that fits comfortably. If you've determined no such thing exists (we can't imagine), find another means of staying in shape that does not so compromise your professional image.

TAKING CARE
OF DRESS SHOES

If shoes are to go the distance, you have to pamper them. We have already mentioned the best plan is to have a minimum of two pairs so one can go while the other dries and rests.

We also mentioned the cedar shoe tree, an investment of less than $20 that will save you much more in the long run. If you can't afford cedar shoe trees, wads of newspaper will do. Put them inside your shoes as soon as you take them off. Shoes will regain and retain original shape. Leave shoes out (not in a box) so air can circulate around them. They dry best this way.

Just as a professional laundering is money well spent for shirts, a professional shoe shine is also a worthy investment. Keep a soft cloth, a brush, and polish at home for emergencies, but trust major upkeep to a trained professional. The shine will look great and last longer.

How often shoes need shining depends on wear and weather. Check them out carefully each morning. Get them polished sooner rather than later.

All suede shoes need is a good brushing. A suede brush is available anywhere shoe care supplies are sold. You don't need to do this after every wearing, unless they're particularly dirty. Every few months is fine.

It's not our intention to overwhelm with details, but when it comes to putting together the right image, these things matter.

We will try to make this as quick and painless as possible, giving you only the information you need.

Jewelry

This is easy: Less is more. None is better. This, of course, does not include the necessary watch, cuff links or wedding band.

Beyond those, however, man—especially a young one—is better off without jewelry. No bracelets, collar pins, tie tacks, tie clips, visible necklaces, or rings, even college rings. Some signet-type school rings aren't bad, but they're not great, either.

Stones, diamonds especially, look showy on young men (older men, too), so nix those.

And if we even have to mention that anything pierced should be concealed or, better still, allowed to grow back, then we have larger issues than we thought.

The best cuff link is small and unobtrusive. No larger than a dime. Nothing cutesy or obvious. Double-sided links connected by a chain are classic, but they're more difficult to thread than the little flip-bar type. Compromise by getting a double-link connected with a solid bar. A plain metal knot—gold or silver—is a good choice, and inexpensive fabric knots in a quiet color to complement shirts are acceptable. A small, plain oval is also tasteful.

Watches

Every man should wear a watch. To be without indicates the wearer is unprepared, disorganized, and lacking punctuality.

The watch should also be authentic. No fake Rolex, please. But a Rolex-style is OK, as long as it's not trying too hard to mimic the real thing. For example, several manufacturers make a quality stainless steel diving watch. That's fine. A plain rectangular-faced tank watch with black leather strap is another classic. It, too, is a good choice.

Pocket watches and a chain with a vested suit can be very elegant.

One note: Whatever watch you choose, it must be analog. No digital readouts, calculators, or strange alarms going off at inopportune times.

Socks

Heave a huge sigh of relief. You can get by with nothing but black socks, either over the calf or mid-calf. If you can afford a little variety, match the sock to suit: Black with charcoal gray. Navy with navy. But you can't go wrong with black socks.

The only other thing you need to know is these black socks, also known as "hosiery," should be relatively thin. Not see-through thin, but thin.

If you live in a cold climate, wool is fine as long as it's a fine wool (get it?). Otherwise, acrylic, cotton, or a blend is good. Nothing shiny.

Make sure they cover the leg well up the calf and have good elasticity to stay up. The subtle ribbing found in many men's dress socks helps them stay up. That's good. When they start to wrinkle down over the foot, toss them. Avoid loud patterns. Your socks should be very quiet.

Belt

Again, a quality black leather belt with simple, open, thin metal buckle is the ticket.

You can get by with lesser quality in a leather belt than you can in, say, shoes. But if it's glued, rather than stitched, to its lining and materials are really inferior, it may not wear well. Edges should be smooth and even.

Leather should not be too glossy or heavily textured. Lizard and crocodile used to be common in men's dress belts, but price has made that prohibitive. Imitations are everywhere. Steer clear until you can afford authenticity.

Your belt should match your dress shoes. Black with black, brown with brown when you're ready. No exceptions.

Braces

No, not for your teeth. These hold up men's pants. Rather, they used to hold up men's pants. Now braces, aka suspenders, have gone the way of the pocket watch: still classic, but uncommon.

These are not for you, certainly not at this fledgling state of your career. But should you find yourself inexplicably drawn to braces in the future, know that they fasten to special buttons tucked well inside custom-made trousers. They never clip on, and they're never ever worn with a belt.

Wallet

Like shoes, a wallet can be one of those telltale signs. Because it remains hidden most of the time, some men are apt to scrimp. So when the critical time comes for you to pay for the cab or pick up the check and this ancient, tattered, overstuffed, U-shaped thing held together with duct tape emerges from your pocket, eyebrows will be raised.

Although we all wish you a bulging wallet in the figurative sense, understand that sitting on such a thing can lead to back problems. Whether you choose a hip-pocket or breast-pocket style is immaterial. What's important is that it be a quality leather and that it demonstrate just how organized you are on every level. Keep only a few bare essentials in it, so it remains thin and tidy. If you need to carry cash, invest in an unadorned money clip, available at fine jewelry stores everywhere.

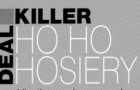

KILLER DEAL HO HO HOSIERY

Like ties, socks are no place for cheer. No clever little candy canes, no cartoon characters, no smiley faces. No one is amused, least of all your clients and boss. If a part of you embraces such socks, save the chuckles for purely social occasions, like watching television with the family.

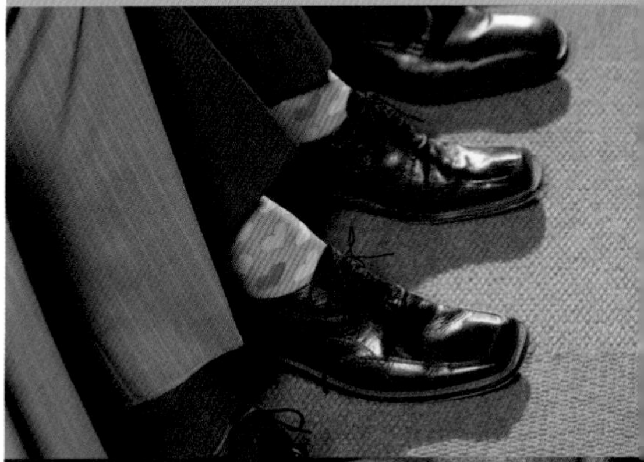

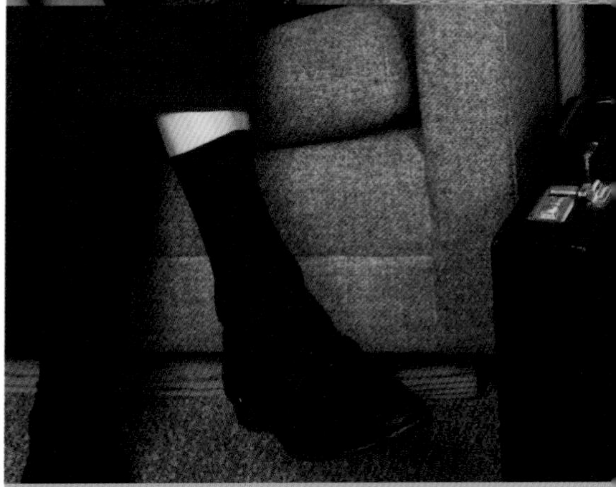

KILLER DEAL TOO MUCH LEG

It's bad enough for the hem of a man's pants to hike up way above his ankles when he sits. It's worse for that same view to show bare leg. In some countries, it's considered downright offensive.

This blunder is easily remedied by purchasing socks that cover the calf, aptly called "over-the-calf hose."

Briefcase

The style of briefcase you choose should be driven mostly by its use. If you rely on a laptop, it will be a laptop carrier. If you travel frequently and need a portable desk, it should be hard-shelled. If you have to tote mounds of paper, a larger capacity softside is appropriate. If you're only carrying a few documents, a slim underarm leather envelope is fine. All are acceptable.

Style of briefcase matters less than quality. Whatever the style, it should be leather, as fine a grade as you can afford. Its color should match the shoes and belt you wear most often, which for now is black. Don't ignore wear and tear: If the briefcase looks beaten up, you may, too.

As important as what's on the outside is what's inside. The briefcase is much like the wallet in this way. What is or isn't inside says a lot about the man carrying it. If it's overloaded, disorganized, or badly in need of a good cleaning out, its carrier is probably similarly guilty. Neat, organized, focused on the essentials? Ditto.

Whatever you do, don't go into meetings outside the office carrying a naked legal pad, loose papers, or whatever it is you require. Nor should you haul a big briefcase around with only three ballpoint pens and a notebook in it. The first appears unprofessional, the second self-important. Invest in a slim leather envelope or notebook and use it.

Pens

Most men don't think of a pen as an accessory, but it's one of those little touches that can make a great impression. We don't suggest you rush out and spend your first paycheck on a fine Waterman or Mont Blanc. We do suggest you purchase a supply of quality, unadorned, capped ink pens in a nonplastic-looking finish, black ink only. This way you won't wind up taking notes with some funky free pen featuring a competitor's corporate logo, nor will you risk irritating anyone by mindlessly clicking a ballpoint during meetings. Keep two of your pens on you at all times. Be prepared to offer one to your client, your boss, the woman wanting to share her phone number. Tell them to keep it. People remember these things.

Cell phone

Ha! Gotcha. Irrespective of the fact the cell phone has become an appendage as common as the nose, it is not, nor should it ever be, an accessory. In public, the cell phone should be neither seen nor heard—and most certainly not worn. No nifty leather cases attached to belts, no clips to pants pockets, no strange wires dangling from ears, and no headsets. If you must be in touch constantly, tuck the phone discreetly in a pocket and switch it to "vibrate."

Umbrella

Wanted: One quality folded sturdy black umbrella. Must be willing to travel. Nothing cheap. This baby has to take wind, weather, and revolving doors in stride. No logos, no patterns, no slogans, no multicolored golf varieties. Polished solid wood handle, hooked to hang on the back of a chair. Standard manual opening mechanism (no one needs malfunction in a downpour).

Carry it always, especially on suspicious days. You may be someone's hero.

Dress hats

There's an old saying about how you never forget a woman in a hat. Be careful the same doesn't apply to you. If it's certifiably frigid outside, a dark felt or wool fedora is acceptable, as long as you park it as soon as you get inside the office.

Scarves

Wool scarves can be very handsome not to mention toasty, tucked in the neck of an overcoat. But they are not to be worn without an overcoat. They should never be a suit accessory. That is for women only.

Resist loud patterns, overly long proportions, dangly fringe, and bulky, itchy wools. Choose quietly contrasting solids (deep reds) and subtle tone-on-tone dark plaids that are soft to the touch. Cashmere is the best. But if you can't afford it, some inexpensive acrylics do a reasonable imitation.

The silk scarf is best avoided. Although some silks add an elegant touch with a topcoat, beware the color and shine. White is out of the question unless with a tuxedo. You don't want to come off as some wannabe opera singer.

Gloves

A leather glove for cold weather adds both elegance and warmth. Black is the first choice, assuming your overcoat is navy, charcoal gray, or black. Chocolate brown is also viable with navy and is preferred with a camel or khaki top coat.

Gloves can be lined or unlined, depending on the climate. But they should be real leather with nice, tight seams and no obvious decoration.

Note that gloves should only be worn with an overcoat. Wearing gloves with just a suit looks like you're out to commit a crime.

Eyeglasses

Contact lenses and advanced surgery have erased this dilemma for many men. But those whose vision challenges can't be solved thusly need to be extremely careful about selecting frames. We can't resist saying it's easy to make a spectacle of yourself with frames that are too large, too small, or ill-shaped for your face and head. Too large and you're Mr. Peepers. Too small and you look like John Lennon in the Yoko years. You get the idea.

The best advice is to seek out a frame shop with professionals who will give you yes/no advice. Ask the salesperson to tell you the shape of your face (this is a test) and if the answer is right, he or she gets to make recommendations.

In general, pupils should be in the center of the frame and eyebrows should be close to the top of the frame. Stay away from bold shiny metal rims, as they look like jewelry. Small metal frames, however, can be elegant. Black plastic frames look Elvis Costello–strange. High-fashion extremes are out, as is anything bearing a designer's logo. Gravitate towards classics like rimless or some variation of tortoiseshell. For good measure, wear your suit when trying on glasses.

Always have two pairs in your current prescription that look good. They can even be identical, if that makes you happy. If one pair breaks or gets lost, resorting to some funky old pair or—dare we even say it?—performing a paper-clip/safety-pin temporary fix-it is not an option.

A word of caution on lenses: Never tint them for indoor wear. Don't even go for those gradiant indoor/outdoor lenses. Shading makes you look shady.

Be equally mindful of sensible style when picking out sunglasses. Subdued, dude. The UV resistance provides essential protection for your eyes, but whip shades off the minute—the *minute*—you enter a building. Your future is not that bright.

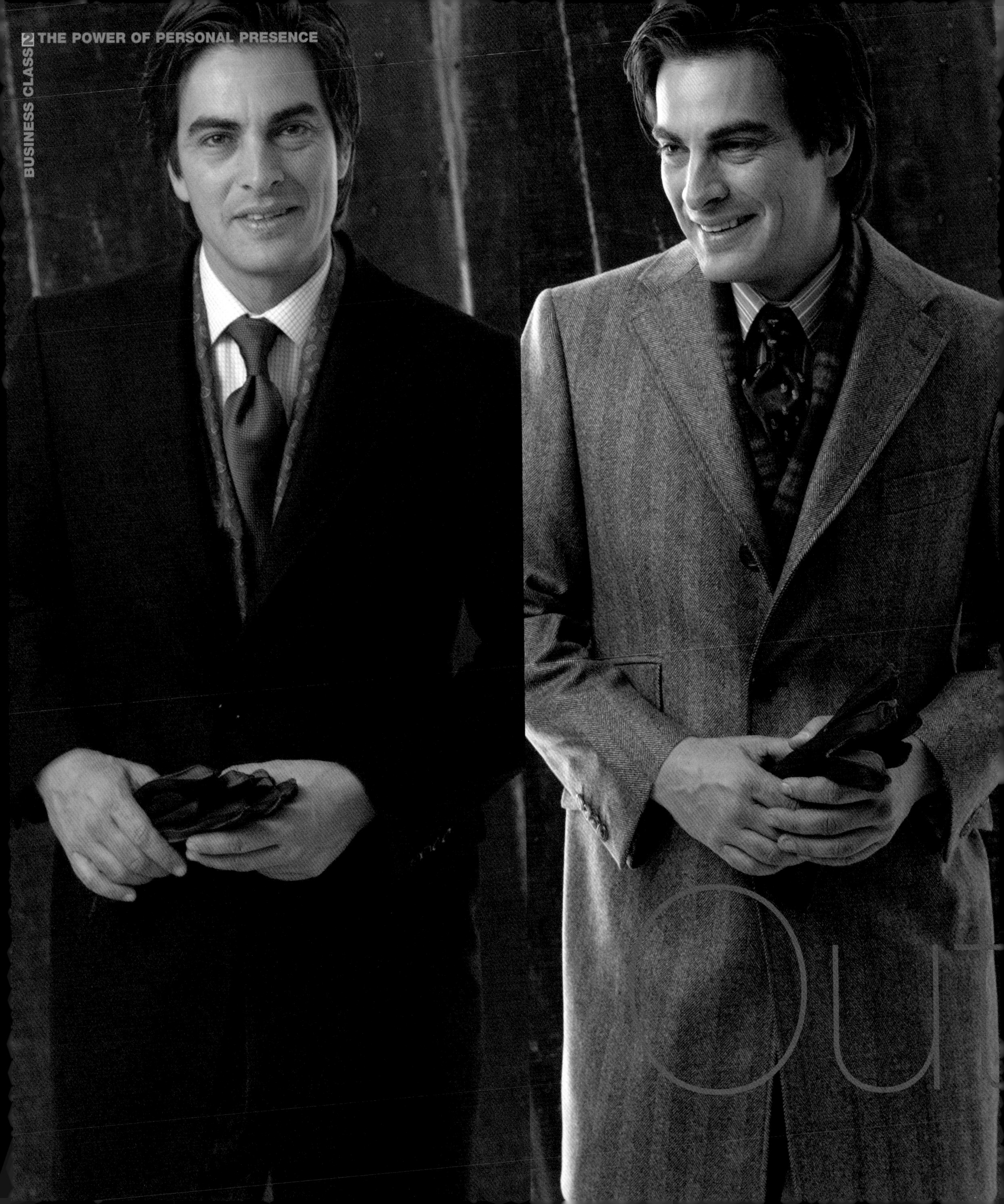
Out

Even if sunny Southern California is home base, big business always means face-to-face meetings in cold weather cities like New York, Washington, or Paris. Don't get caught without a suitable coat. It makes you look unprepared and uncomfortable, which is not what potential clients and partners like to see.

Every man needs a topcoat to wear over suits. **Invest in a full-length dark navy, black, or charcoal gray coat.** The fabric should be a natural wool, as rich as you can afford and as warm as you need. Cashmere is the ultimate. Get as close as possible.

When judging quality, think of it as another suit coat. Look at seams, buttons and buttonholes, rear vent, and the lay of the collar and lapels. Topcoats should look as crisply tailored as a suit.

The fit should be equally refined. The ideal is generous enough to slide easily over the suit, but not so oversized that you look like a five-year-old in Daddy's coat. The sleeves should be longer than either your suit or shirt sleeves by a half-inch. Don't let them hang down over your hands (again, the kid thing), but do cover your wrists entirely.

The hem length hits just below the knee to somewhere around mid-calf. Any shorter and it becomes a three-quarter length car coat.

Secondary color choices for topcoats are certain dark tweeds and camel. None of these has the presence of navy, but a wool camel or real camel hair is considered a classic. A dark coat is most serviceable in the long run, however.

erwear

Raincoats

Even if you have a topcoat, you also need a raincoat. The most common cuts for distinguished raincoats are the trench or a balmacaan. The former is double-breasted with a yoke, epaulets, and a belt, or some combination thereof. The latter is single-breasted with raglan sleeves and a small rounded collar. Most come in some shade of tan, beige, or khaki, which makes them suitable year-round. Fabric is usually cotton twill or wool gabardine. Leather is out of the question, unless you're an aspiring loan shark, pimp, or thug.

Taller men can wear either trench or balmacaan. Shorter men are better off in the balmacaan because it's less cluttered.

If you do go for the trench, mind the belt. If weather warrants wearing the coat buttoned and belted, tie the fabric belt in a knot around your waist so there are two even ends hanging. If you buckle the belt, one long end flops aimlessly and looks silly.

If you don't use the belt, knot it the same way around the back so it's not flapping around. Whatever you do, don't remove the belt. Empty loops look like you lost something. Who wants to look like a loser?

{ Tip: If you're not apt to wear the topcoat often, a classic full-length raincoat with a zip-out lining may suffice for business dress. It's not as polished as the wool topcoat and certainly won't go over your tuxedo at night, but it's better than shivering. }

DEAL KILLER
DOWN IS OUT

It's cold, dress coats are expensive, and you have a perfectly good green down parka with a hood in the closet. Don't even think about it.

Jackets are meant for casual and recreational wear. Putting one over a suit is like the Boston Red Sox wearing tux jackets over their uniforms. It doesn't work. It defeats the purpose of the outfit in both form and function.

Find a way to get a full-length coat, even if it means searching secondhand resources for a quality pre-owned model. Repeat the mantra: Dress to the position you want, not the position you have.

The Executiv Ward

Once a man's level of success allows him to expand his suit wardrobe, he encounters a veritable treasure trove of sumptuous fabric and handsome variation. Although good sense may dictate staying within the realm of conservative dress, how he executes that conservatism steps up a notch or three or four. He can now afford to incorporate touches of personal style. Things get interesting. This is not about being eccentric—although there are those for whom stand-out signature dressing has proven effective. It is more about refining one's wardrobe with carefully selected additions.

Simply put, the more successful a man becomes, the more choices he has—in dressing as in life. Many men collect dozens of suits with both winter and summer wardrobes.

The following sections highlight some of those choices. Everything that has been established up to now still applies. The rules of what's acceptable don't change, but they do bend for those whose experience speaks for itself. Here is where you come to understand the difference between a $700 suit and a $3,000 suit (or even double that price), a custom-made shirt and a factory-made shirt, a wool blazer and a cashmere blazer.

For the young man, it gives a taste of what's to come. For those who are already there, it offers possibilities for making the wardrobe more enjoyable.

The Suit

CONTINUING TO BUILD YOUR TOM JAMES WARDROBE

Earlier in this chapter, we outlined the first five suits a young man entering professional life should own. Assuming the seasoned executive's wardrobe already contains those five suits, we suggest five more suits to round out the selection.

The next five suits
- A navy herringbone
- A solid or small pattern in medium brown or olive
- A medium gray muted check or plaid
- A tan or taupe solid
- A black and white mini-check or Prince of Wales plaid

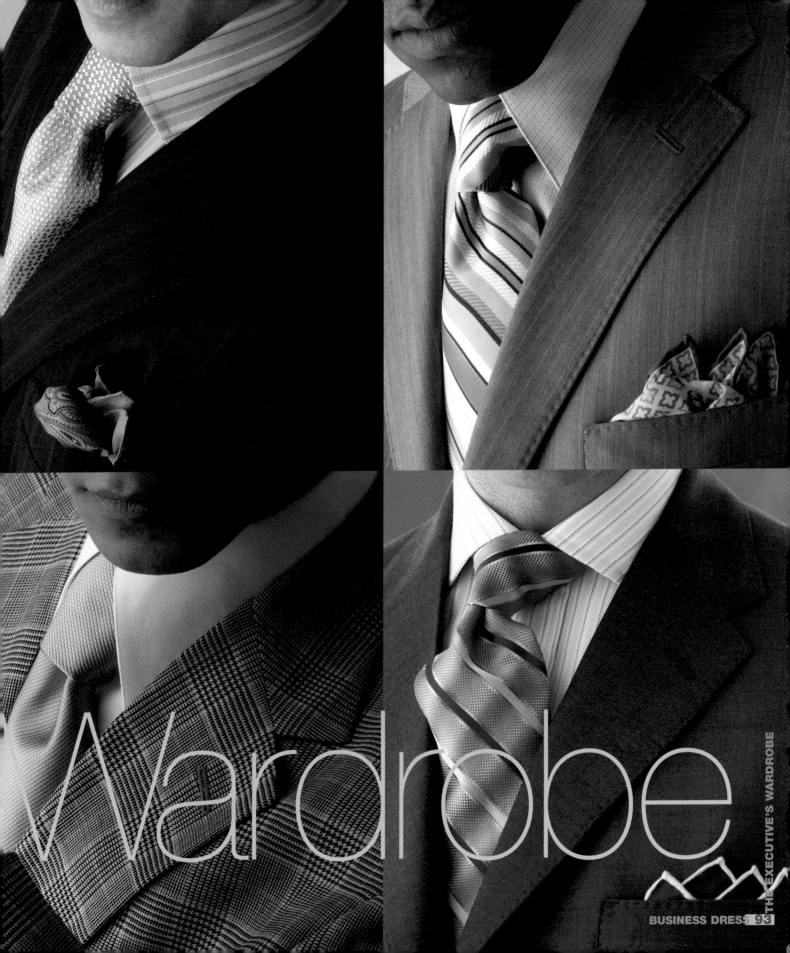

Wardrobe

QUALITY

At this stage, it is not enough simply to know what suit color and fabric to own. The elements of higher quality also come into play.

Two basic elements distinguish the suits one buys before and after arriving at a certain station. Those elements are tailoring and fabric.

Whereas the first suits discussed earlier in this chapter are likely to be ready-made—or, in clothing industry jargon, "off the rack"—we now move into "made to measure" suits. These may also be called "custom-made" or "tailor-made." These suits are made expressly for the customer, allowing him to select the fabric from a vast array of swatches and to receive the finest fit and custom detailing.

The following section offers the discriminating gentleman a detailed look at what constitutes a fine suit.

Structure

From the Tom James company manual on what determines a well-made suit structurally:

"**Stitching:** Look for signs of handwork (uneven but tighter stitching) in the shoulders and lapels. The more stitches per inch, the stronger the seam. Hand-stitched garments, sewn at stress seams with 100 percent silk thread, drape with a more natural shape, allow more freedom of movement, and have more lasting durability. At the junction where sleeve and shoulder meet, watch out for rippling or unnecessary gathering. The tension of the stitches needs to be tight, but not so tight that the seam does not lie flat and straight. Sleeves should conform to the arms naturally, and the lapels should roll naturally rather than have a sharp crease. The distance of stitching from edges should be consistent throughout the coat.

Interfacing: All jackets have an inner chest piece that gives the front of the jacket shape and rigidity, but too much stiffness can give a jacket a slightly unnatural look. A quality jacket has either a soft woven fusible front, or in the finest jackets, a "floatable" canvas front that is sewn in by hand. Squeeze the material over the chest to see if it is soft and resilient. The interfacing should provide the true feel of the shell fabric, not the rigid touch of the inner structure. The more your client wears a suit with quality interfacing, the better it conforms to his body, holds its shape, resists wrinkles, and withstands the rigors of many dry cleanings.

Collar: Turn the collar of the jacket inside out and look for a flat flannel lining, evenly sewn with small, neat stitches. This ensures that the collar will lie flat against the neck and retain that shape through long wear. A machine-sewn collar will not hug the neck evenly or maintain its shape through the process of wearing and dry cleaning.

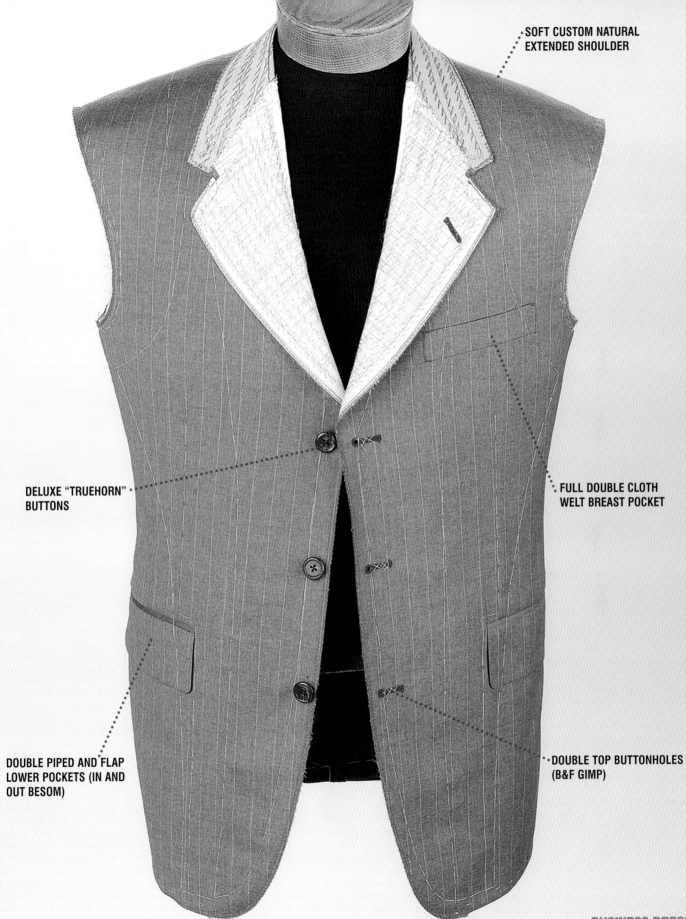

SOFT CUSTOM NATURAL
EXTENDED SHOULDER

FULL DOUBLE CLOTH
WELT BREAST POCKET

DELUXE "TRUEHORN"
BUTTONS

DOUBLE TOP BUTTONHOLES
(B&F GIMP)

DOUBLE PIPED AND FLAP
LOWER POCKETS (IN AND
OUT BESOM)

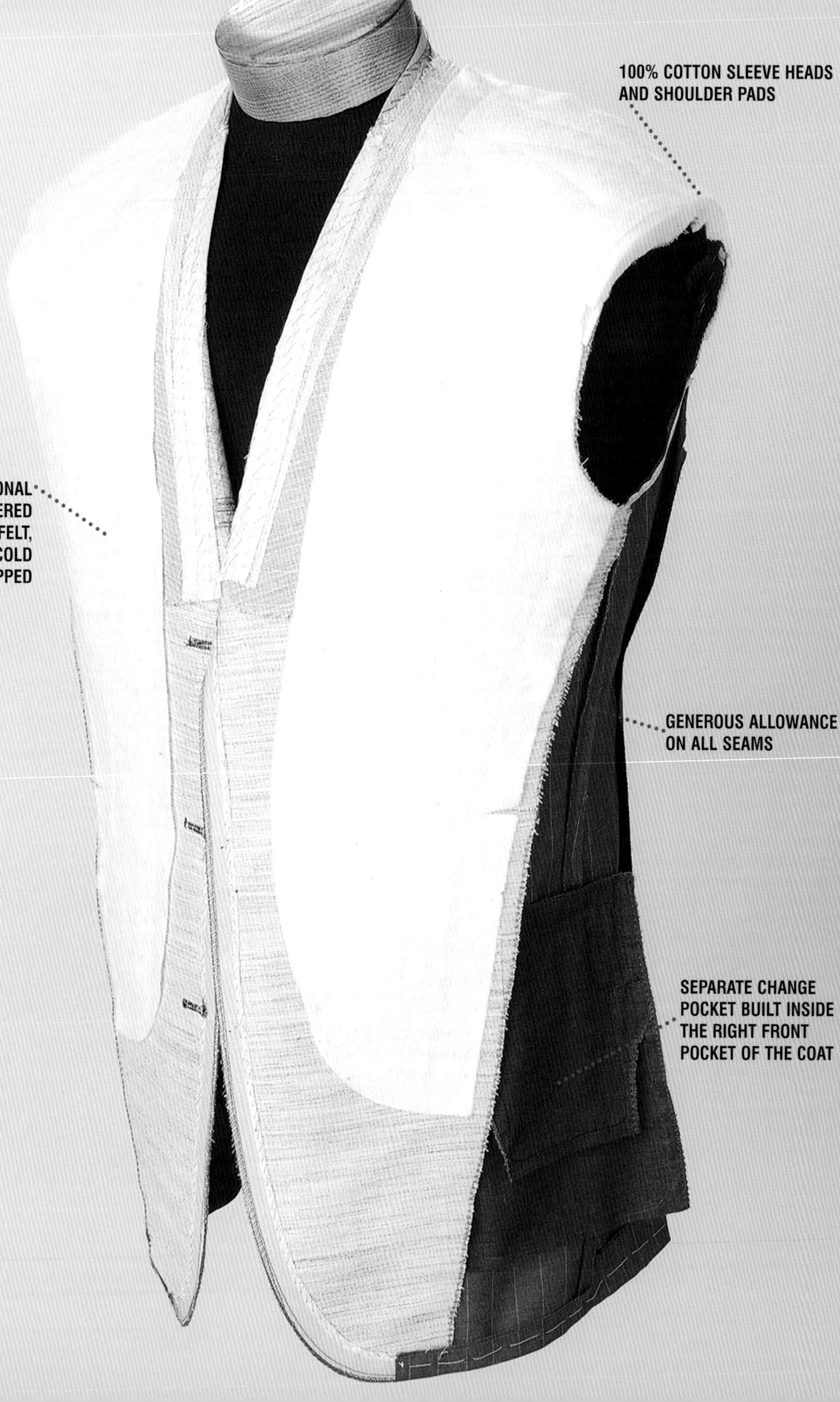

100% COTTON SLEEVE HEADS
AND SHOULDER PADS

SOFT, FULL CONVENTIONAL
CANVAS FRONT COVERED
WITH 100% FLANNEL FELT,
PRESHRUNK AND COLD
WATER DIPPED

GENEROUS ALLOWANCE
ON ALL SEAMS

SEPARATE CHANGE
POCKET BUILT INSIDE
THE RIGHT FRONT
POCKET OF THE COAT

Armholes: Armhole seams should be notched according to the slope of the shoulder to prevent stretching and distortion. Look for hand-sewn, double-layered functional arm shields, which are small pieces of lining material sewn under the armhole inside the jacket to protect the fabric and lining from minor perspiration stains and odor.

Lining: The jacket lining should be silky smooth so there will be no tug or friction when you put on the jacket over a shirt or sweater. The best material is 100 percent Cupra Bemberg, a brand name for a synthetic fabric that is as smooth as silk but stronger and more durable. The body and sleeve lining should be individually fit and cut for each garment.

Pattern: If the suit has any pattern, look carefully at every place where the material is sewn. All patterns should be fully matched up, down and across—matched at the side, back, and shoulder seams; sleeves matched to the front of the coat; top sleeve matched to the under sleeve across the back; the collar matched to the center back; each lapel and pocket flap matched to the other. The best manufacturers plot and trace patterns for each garment by computer and cut by laser directly on the fabric for accuracy that far exceeds that of the human hand. If the entire coat is not balanced, that is an immediate tip-off to poor workmanship and an attempt to save material.

Alteration: Check to be sure that generous seam allowances are provided to enable the suit to be properly adjusted if the wearer adds a few pounds. Inspect the jacket along the seams and check the trousers to be sure there is sufficient fabric in the seat, crotch, and leg for necessary alterations and a comfortable fit. A quality suit will allow altering the garment up or down two full sizes.

Buttons: All buttons should be of genuine horn content, which gives them durability and strength and adds a rich luster to the appearance. Check to be sure buttons are set close together, their edges 'kissing.' Buttonholes should be firmly attached and stitched evenly with no loose threads.

Trousers: Trouser features to check include a true French fly for extra support; a full band roll in the waistband to provide comfort and prevent waistband curl with belt or braces; belt loops sewn into the waistband (not tacked on) for a nicer look and stronger performance; an open center back (breather pleat) that allows the waistband to expand after a meal and open and close while moving; a nickel-plated brass zipper for durability and a cleaner appearance; bar tacks on all stress points to prevent opening of seams and give extra support to pockets, crotch, seat, and thigh areas; and pocketing of 100 percent cotton for sturdiness and durability."

BRACER BUTTONS SEWN INTO TROUSER

TRUE FRENCH FLY

REINFORCED BACK CROTCH PIECE

SECRET INSIDE POCKET WITH FLAP

FRONT OF TROUSERS ARE LINED TO THE KNEE

DETAILS

A custom suit also offers the option of including certain details. They are as follows:

FUNCTIONAL BUTTONHOLES: Sleeve buttons that actually button and unbutton are a popular hand-tailored feature and a sure sign of a custom garment.

/16TH HAND-STITCHED EDGES: This is a very light stitch done on the edges of coat lapels, besom flaps, and pocket welt. It is done completely by hand and finishes the look with a definite custom silhouette.

BEYOND THE ADVANTAGES OF SUPERIOR CONSTRUCTION AND DETAIL, A CUSTOM SUIT AFFORDS IMPECCABLE FIT. THIS IS ESPECIALLY IMPORTANT FOR THE MAN WHOSE PROPORTIONS MAY NOT MATCH THOSE OF THE AVERAGE OFF-THE-RACK SUIT MODEL. CUSTOM TAILORING ALLOWS FOR BROADER SHOULDERS, LONGER TORSO, PROMINENT SEAT, DIFFERENCES IN POSTURE—WHATEVER YOUR PARTICULAR NEEDS MAY BE.

SIDE VENTS: Side vents on a suit or sports coat are not something one will likely see on a store-bought suit. Side vents are a British influence, and the look is timeless.

OUTSIDE TICKET POCKET: A smaller ticket pocket on the outside of the jacket just above the right side coat pocket gives a suit or sports coat a sportier custom look. This is a throwback to the romantic era of the 1920s and '30s that used British styling as their inspiration.

PATCH POCKETS: Since patch pockets add another layer to the jacket's surface, they are considered the most casual of the three classic suit pockets (the three being patch, flap, and the dressiest, besom). Patch pockets (just side pockets, or side pockets and breast pocket) complement the sportier or light-colored solid suit or sports coat.

VEST: Because of the additional cost, vests are seldom found with an off-the-rack suit, so this, too, is a custom look. Vests can be double-breasted or single-breasted and can be made with or without lapels, originally part of every suit.

TROUSER DETAILING: Top, half, or cord pockets at the front, flap pockets at the rear, and wider one-half to 1 inch belt loops (or no loops and extension waistband if trousers will be worn only with braces) add interest and give trousers more of a custom look to cover a gentleman's waistband for modesty

FABRIC

The other mark of a fine suit is its extraordinary fabric. Although most men choosing custom will continue to opt for a year-round 100 percent wool, the properties of that wool can be vastly superior to the less costly variety. How one wool is distinguished from another begins with the animal from which it is sheared and continues on through every step of its refining process. Those steps are outlined here.

Sheep are reared in nearly every country in the world, and many are bred to grow finer, thinner hairs. Because of their special mixture of climate and other natural resources, New Zealand and Tasmania produce some of the finest wool in the world. Three-quarters of the sheep of Australia, the world's largest producer of fine wool, are merinos, and the fibers of merino wool are so fine that a string of them a mile long would weigh only 0.01 ounce. These are milled in the Holland & Sherry mill in Tome, Chile.

After sheep are sheared, fibers are sorted in a highly skilled manual process involving sight and touch. The sorter looks for luster and waviness and feels for density and strength. However, the most important quality difference between fleeces is the average fiber fineness, or diameter. The finer that hair, the finer the wool quality.

The wool sorter's matchings are given quality numbers: 100s, 110s, 120s, and so on. The higher the number the finer (more delicate) and expensive the cloth will be. The higher numbers are for special occasion clothing. The quality numbers applied to fibers are also defined by diameter measured in microns. For instance, a super 80 fabric will have a fiber fineness of 19.5 microns, whereas a super 130 fabric will have a fiber fineness of only 17.0 microns. The finer super 180s wool will have the nicer feel and drape and, because it is more rare, will be more expensive, but cannot be worn as often or as many times. If you are still building your suit wardrobe, you may want to buy super 100s, not the higher numbers like 120s, 140s, 160s, or 180s.

MICRON 100S CHART

SUPER 200s weighted mean value μ > 13.26 < 13.75

SUPER 190s weighted mean value μ > 13.76 < 14.25

SUPER 180s weighted mean value μ > 14.26 < 14.75

SUPER 170s weighted mean value μ > 14.76 < 15.25

SUPER 160s weighted mean value μ > 15.26 < 15.75

SUPER 150s weighted mean value μ > 15.76 < 16.25

SUPER 140s weighted mean value μ > 16.26 < 16.75

SUPER 130s weighted mean value μ > 16.76 < 17.25

SUPER 120s weighted mean value μ > 17.26 < 17.75

SUPER 110s weighted mean value μ > 17.76 < 18.25

SUPER 100s weighted mean value μ > 18.26 < 18.75

That said, not all super 100s or super 120s are created equally. The quality of the raw wool may be the same grade or fineness, but how it is milled goes a long way in determining how the finished garment will look, feel, and perform. Milling includes scouring, blending, carding (straightening and untangling fibers), combing, drawing (reducing thickness to an untwisted thread having about fifty fibers in its cross-section), and spinning.

While spinning wool into high quality yarns, "twist" (stated in turns per inch) draws the fibers closer together. Two-ply, which is the twisting of two yarns together, produces a stronger fiber that is more resilient and durable.

The weaving process determines whether a fabric is a worsted or a woolen. Worsteds are smoother in texture or appearance and have a crisper hand. Woolens are usually bulkier, more dense, and have a spongy hand. Sometimes, as with tweeds, woolens feel slightly hairy.

Just as natural resources in certain regions can influence the quality of wool fibers produced by sheep, natural resources can influence the quality of finishing techniques. The finest mill in the world is the Holland & Sherry mill in Tome, Chile. This mill produces cloth for Tom James clothing and for other manufacturers of fine clothing around the world. When you select super 100s, 110s, 120s, etc., from your Tom James clothier, you will receive the opportunity to select from the finest cloths in the world.

A Tom James wardrobe

A GLOSSARY

Cashmere hair is combed from goats reared in Central Asia and is named for Kashmir, a mountainous area of India and Pakistan. The goat's fleece is mostly a long, relatively coarse hair, but the underhair, or "duvet," is sleek and silky. Cashmere is luxurious, silky soft to the touch and warm without weight and takes dye better than any other of the rarer wools. Quality can vary considerably, however. The coarser, clipped hair from the back of the goat is technically cashmere, but it is of much poorer quality than hair combed from the duvet.

Camel hair yarns are spun from the fleeces of the camel. These fibers are soft, warm, very lightweight, and less delicate than cashmere. The finest camel hair cloth is the underhair from the Bactrian (two-humped) camel found in the Chinese Highlands. Camel hair's natural color is beige to brownish black, but it can be dyed. The natural camel color has long been popular in blazers and topcoats.

Alpaca yarns are spun from the fleeces of alpacas, which are members of the camel family. Yarns are highly lustrous with softness similar to cashmere. Raised in the Andes Mountains of Chile and Peru, alpacas are domestic animals. The fleeces are usually obtained after a two-year growth.

Vicuna is soft fur from a South American llama-like animal found at elevations as high as 12,000 feet in almost inaccessible regions of Peru, Bolivia, and Ecuador. Its natural color is a rich tobacco shade, and the hair of the neck is the finest and most highly valued. Unlike alpacas, the vicuna runs wild, so the fur can be very hard to come by, adding to its expense. Recently, a method has been discovered for harvesting the fleece without killing the animal, thus making it available in countries where it had been banned.

Mohair is the long, silky hair of the Angora goat. The softest and finest mohair is from the kid Angora goat. It shares wool's insulating properties and is extremely lightweight. South Africa and the United States are the leading producers. Mohair is a very fine, but somewhat brittle fiber, with a very hard finish and a luster. Fibers are very receptive to dye, and colors are especially brilliant. Mohair's crisp, dry feel makes it ideal for summer formalwear and suits. It is blended with fine worsted wool, producing a cloth with less sheen but more softness and drape, as suits made from 100 percent mohair feel harsh and scratchy to the touch.

As a man's wardrobe grows, it may also become segmented by season. While it is prudent to always maintain some year-round-weight wools, the luxury of choice may well include richly textured wools for cold climate wear and linens and silks for warmer days.

Silk yarn is made from the thread-like filaments the silkworm spins around itself to form its cocoon. Yarns are strong; the silk thread is almost as strong as one of equal diameter in steel. Silk is also extremely resilient; a three-foot length stretched to three and one-half feet will subsequently revert to its original length. While silk is not spun from animal hair, it is considered an animal fiber because it has a protein structure. Like animal hair fibers, silk does not conduct heat and is therefore a good insulator, keeping one warm in winter and cool in summer.

Linen fiber is derived from the stem of the flax plant and spun into a lustrous and strong yarn which, like cotton, is extremely comfortable to wear in hot weather, as it draws moisture quickly away from the body. The nature of linen is that it wrinkles easily. Mentioned in the Bible, linen was woven more than 4,000 years ago.

Microfiber, popular today in trousers, is not actually a fiber at all, but rather a new process for making virtually any manufactured synthetic fiber (polyester, nylon, acrylic, rayon). By making the individual fibers very small (about half the diameter of the finest silk), sturdy fabrics can be created that drape well, repel moisture, resist wrinkles, and hold a crease without being stiff.

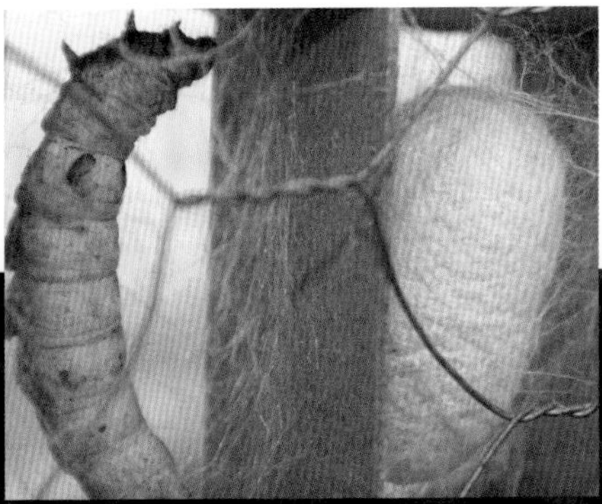

OF FINE WOOLS

A Tom James wardrobe

Executive

Shirts

As with suits, the upscale shirt wardrobe expands according to structure, detail, and fabric.

Most gentlemen will want to move into having their shirts made to ensure the best-looking and most comfortable fit. This also allows for individual preference in details and fabric. No more settling for whatever collar, cuff, and pocket styles happen to come with a ready-made shirt.

A Tom James custom shirt offers a choice of twenty-eight collar styles, ten cuff styles, and eight pocket styles (or no pocket). Quality fabrics include hundreds of choices in solids, stripes, checks, and plaids in a variety of weaves. It's here that a man may incorporate a white collar and cuff on a blue shirt, branch into different collar and cuff styles, embrace more colors and patterns for business attire, and add his monogram to his shirts. A discreet monogram is the mark of a custom-made shirt. Tom James clients can choose from thirty monogram colors in sixteen different styles.

The shirt wardrobe

The ideal wardrobe contains three to four dozen shirts. They are as follows:

- 6 white: 3 regular/3 French cuff
- 6 blue: 3 regular/3 French cuff
- 8 stripes on white or blue background: 2 navy; 3 burgundy or red; 2 tan, yellow, or olive; 2 pink, lavender, or gray
- 8 assorted solids: yellow, cream, pink, lavender, gray (skin tone and suit colors determine choices)
- 2 white background with mini-graph or pin checks: 1 navy, 1 burgundy
- 2 blue background with yellow, navy, or red mini-graph checks
- 3 tuxedo shirts with wing and traditional turn-down collars
- 1 formal white pique with wing collar to wear exclusively with tails

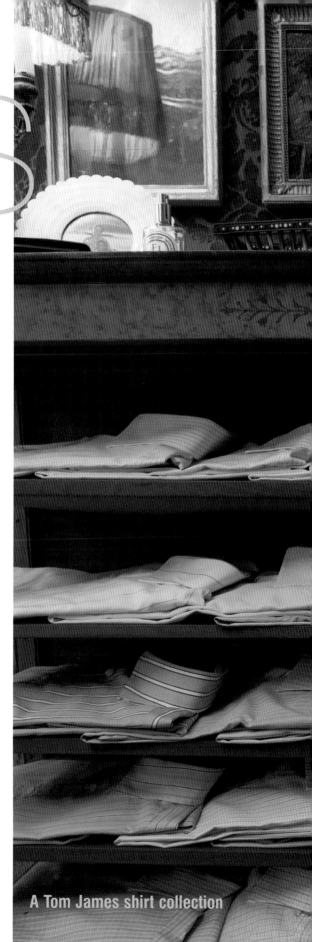

A Tom James shirt collection

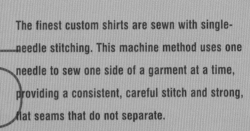

The finest custom shirts are sewn with single-needle stitching. This machine method uses one needle to sew one side of a garment at a time, providing a consistent, careful stitch and strong, flat seams that do not separate.

Other quality points include:

- soft Egyptian cotton interlinings sewn into the collars and cuffs, resulting in a smooth, even appearance and less shrinkage
- sleeve to cuff pleating that gives balance to sleeves and prevents cuffs from turning inward
- double collar beading securing collar leaf to band that gives the collar body and support
- pockets, collars, and cuffs hand set for an exact match both vertically and horizontally for patterned fabrics
- built-in stay pockets to prevent the collar stays from showing through the fabric
- mother of pearl or trocca buttons.

Ties

If a man's business attire were a painting on the wall, the suit would be the frame, the shirt would be the mat, and the tie would be the focal point. Ties provide color and interest, making the rest of the ensemble work. If a man is correctly pulled together, his tie is the one aspect of his appearance everyone notices. It is the statement piece.

The most basic solid and background colors for ties are blues, burgundies, reds, and yellows. Red, yellow, and sometimes other bold colors are especially effective in drawing the eye and commanding a presence, particularly when a man is wearing a white shirt. These are the so-called "power ties."

Vivid color in the pattern also commands a presence. Signal orange, bright green, and other offbeat colors are best restricted to the pattern rather than the ground color of the tie, but as an accent can give a great lift to dark suits.

Because the tie is closest to the face, use the tie's ground color as a powerful tool for offsetting the negative effect of less flattering colors in a suit. For example, a tan suit may not be the best color on a particular individual, but adding a tie with a flattering primary color and design that bring in a small amount of the suit's color can enhance the look.

Solid ties also take on new life as wardrobe quality improves. A combination of solids tends to emphasize the qualities of the materials and tailoring by not giving the eye extraneous details on which to focus.

It is recommended that a man have four neckties with each suit, blazer, and sports coat. Two are hardly enough for the investment one makes in a fine suit or jacket.

As careers become established, some men prefer to move into bow ties for business as a trademark style. Since bow ties are uncommon these days, even in academic circles, they make a memorable impression as a note of eccentricity. If a man embraces that sort of attention, the bow tie remains a classic alternative to the straight tie.

A tie's most tangible asset, its outer silk shell, accounts for about two-thirds of its price. An exceptional tie should possess a rich and sensuous hand (a term describing the fabric's weight, texture, and fall). It should feel supple, not rough, and should lie and drape perfectly flat without bumps or ripples. It should not only be made of finer fabric, but of heavier fabric. Finer, heavier silk not only feels and drapes better, it knots better, too.

Superior color and pattern are also part of the cost. Finer silk fabric takes color better and allows for a higher quantity of silk screens. Shading colors is very complex, sometimes using four screens to show a gradual change in color in better ties. The color will not be as rich, and the complexity of the pattern will not be as intricate, in a less expensive tie. In wovens, more colors in the design mean more different-colored threads were used and, thus, the tie is more expensive.

Another mark of the exceptional tie is its inner lining. This lining is what keeps a tie looking fresh and hanging straight despite multiple knottings and wearings. The finest quality ties are lined with 100 percent wool, and the weight of the lining is carefully varied with the shell fabric to provide the most uniform knot possible. The cushion that fine inner lining provides should be tangible.

A well-made tie has the fabric and interlining connected by something called the slip stitch. This is one continuous thread that allows the fabric and inner lining to move and relax together. The fact that the tie can move along this thread means you can tie a necktie into a knot, remove it, and hang it up, and it will return to its original shape every time. The slip stitch also keeps the tie from ripping when it's wrapped tightly around the neck.

The finest ties should have a loop made from the shell fabric hand-stitched into the center seam. This loop provides a place through which to slide the small end of the tie to hold it in place.

Finally, characteristic of a top-of-the-line tie is silk tip lining. Not to be confused with inner lining, this decorative lining should be the same as the shell fabric or at least in a complementary shade of silk. Like the face of the tie, the tip lining is hand pressed, measured throughout the manufacturing process, and has clean, even margins.

The expanding business wardrobe demands a wider variety of shoes. Many men believe that one style of dress shoe transcends many occasions. This simply is not true for the well-dressed executive.

For formal business, the best choice is a conservative lace-up (wing-tip, cap-toe, cap-toe with medallion) that is worn only with a suit. Other options with a suit that can also be worn less formally include split-toes, monk-straps, and dress loafers. For suits, a five-shoe wardrobe is recommended: two pairs black, two brown, one cordovan in burnished calfskin, shell cordovan, and perhaps even an exotic leather like alligator or lizard.

Wearing braces instead of a belt, dabbling in exotic leathers instead of smooth ones for belts and briefcases, favoring a more prominent cuff link, and choosing more vibrant colors for pocket squares are just a few of the ways the executive assortment wardrobe can be made more interesting. The choices are endless.

Executive

Accesso

ries

THE EXECUTIVE'S WARDROBE

Business

Not so long ago, the words "business casual" would have been an oxymoron. A man dressed for either but never both—unless a game of golf qualifies as "business casual."

Thanks to the 1990s, however, many men are faced with fitting into a less structured dress code without tarnishing their image. They may like the comfort of an open collar, but few embrace the uncertainty of broader choice when the wrong one can spell disaster.

No need to despair. Like dressing for business, a few simple guidelines will keep the young professional out of harm's way.

Just remember this: Should you wake up with the urge to experiment on a casual Friday morning, make an omelet. Creative mistakes in the kitchen can always be dumped down the disposal. Creative mistakes in one's closet become much more public and, therefore, not so quickly disposed.

While corporate dictates vary, what never varies is good sense. Good sense tells us never to push the envelope. It is always better to be overdressed than underdressed, especially in business situations. Even though "casual" is part of the wording, "business" remains operative. You are always—*always*—expected to look like a working professional.

With that in mind, we offer some basic tenets. We have chosen to do this by showing more than telling, because to describe all the many possibilities for business casual would exhaust us all.

Besides, setting a good example always speaks louder than words.

Casual

THE FORMAL "SUIT" INFORMAL

Suit, no tie

This is the dressiest casual look and consists of a transitional suit with dress shirt open at the collar. A transitional suit is defined by fabric: either a textured solid or a subtle pattern such that the trousers could be worn alone as slacks. Examples of such fabrics are bird's-eyes, tic weaves, twills, or mini-checks. These are good for travel because they can be dressed up with shirt and tie or dressed down with a three-button polo or mock turtleneck knit for business casual or social evenings.

Whether or not you are wearing a tie, the suit accessories are the same: quiet leather belt, dress shoe, cuff link.

There is a caveat here: Although the suit-without-tie look is listed here as dressiest, that doesn't mean it is the safest business casual choice. In some circles, a suit—especially a dark solid—worn without a tie comes off as roguish. The safer choice is a navy blazer or tasteful sports coat, wool slacks, and dress shirt.

Navy blazer

The navy blazer is the basis of a great casual wardrobe, business or otherwise. It's fabulous with dress shirts and ties, sport shirts, polos, or with jeans and a good T-shirt for weekend wear. The blazer solves many dilemmas and gets you out of numerous clothing quandaries.

Like the navy suit, the blazer looks good on everyone. Well, the right blazer does. One that is ill-fitting, poorly constructed, or the wrong design doesn't count. As with buying a suit or any other tailored piece of clothing, you must mind the usual quality points. More on that in a moment.

You may have grown up thinking the double-breasted navy blazer with gold buttons is the ultimate in sophistication. News flash: This isn't the blazer for you. You are not yachting. You are working. Like the double-breasted suit, this blazer comes off as too fashion-forward for a young man. The single-breasted model is a much better choice. It's more flexible, less pretentious.

For now, select the highest quality 100 percent worsted wool blazer you can afford. Like your first suit, this fabric will serve you year-round. The buttons can be brass, horn, or something else dark and unobtrusive. They may be stamped with a small pattern, but should not be too ornate or shiny.

Sports coats

Beyond the basic navy blazer, a sports coat in either earth tones, gray tones, blue tones, or a black-and-white pattern works well. This mixed pattern should be ever so subtle, so the overall effect is almost solid. Stick with a two- or three-button single-breasted style, but it can have a slightly softer appearance. A soft roll to the lapel and a slightly less structured shoulder affect this.

The fabric can be a lightweight flannel, twill, or subtle herringbone, for example, to lend a less formal, more touchable look.

Don't confuse this with a rumpled or unstructured look. Sports coats and blazers should be as finely constructed, fitted, and polished as a suit jacket, just not as formal in appearance.

Trousers

A trouser in a medium to dark gray worsted wool is the next staple. It works with the blazer or sports coat or stands alone with a sport shirt. This neutral navy-over-gray palette gives you plenty of leeway to introduce color in your shirt or tie, if you wear one. It also doesn't show dirt, so it's great for travel.

The trouser can be either a plain, flat-front style with straight leg and usually no cuff, or pleated and cuffed. Just make sure the pant isn't cut too generously. Baggy can look messy and bottom-heavy beneath the thinner silhouette of a sport shirt or blazer.

Trousers should always have belt loops—no beltless variations for business.

Colorwise, an alternative to gray trousers is something in the tan family. The navy-blazer-cotton-khaki-pants ensemble is certainly fail-safe, but it's also too safe. It smacks of old habits and college dress. You're a professional now.

Try a fresher variation on this theme with a light wool gabardine trouser in a richer tan shade like toast or camel. The pant will have a more elegant drape and the color a far more interesting impact.

Trousers are not the place for color. Primaries like green and red may coordinate with a navy blazer, but they belong only on the golf course.

Shirt

The best-looking route to business casual is the long-sleeved sport shirt or dress shirt with collar open. The reason we like this is the same reason we insist on long-sleeved dress shirts: Bare arms may feel cool, but they aren't cool. Since most men take off their jackets in the office, blazers and sports coats included, the sport shirt has you covered.

Another advantage of the sport shirt is that it is designed to be worn with the collar open. The collar will likely hold its shape. That's not always the case with dress shirts intended to be worn with ties.

Many sport shirts have collars that button down. These are worn by men who would never wear a button-down collared dress shirt. This is fine.

Sport shirts open up the spectrum for color and pattern. In general, the quieter, the better.

The idea is to look like you intend to do business, not host a luau. Obviously, if your sports jacket sports pattern, your shirt should be solid.

Another acceptable choice can be the three-button knit polo shirt beneath a sports jacket or blazer. As with most items of clothing, not all polo shirts are the same and not all are suitable for the professional. In general, it should look like you bought it for professional wear, not for the golf course. That means no bright colors, no faded colors, no rumpled collars, no logo (unless it is your company's).

The dressiest polos for warm weather are made out of a fine, flat knit like Sea Island cotton, Pima cotton, or silk. For winter, a wool knit or blend looks good. In either season, make sure the knit is not so thin that it exposes you if you take off your jacket. Everyone at the gym may admire your pecs. Everyone at the office will not.

Crewneck and mock turtleneck knit shirts are also sometimes seen as part of business casual looks. We recommend neither in the short-sleeved style, since both come perilously close to being T-shirts. Shirts with traditional collars are the better choice.

> { Tip: Pleats make a trouser feel more comfortable and drape better when a man sits. But they may not make a man look thinner. More billow can make the wearer look more ample. }

DEAL KILLER
TELLING TAILS

Fashion may have sanctioned the appearance of the shirttail outside the pants, but it is never appropriate for a professional look. Not even beneath a sports jacket (*especially* underneath a sports jacket). Not even if the shirttail is squared off and intended to be worn out. Your buds may think it's cool, but older, very successful clients may not.

Always tuck in your shirt and wear a belt. Belt loops without a belt look like you forgot something. If you forgot something this obvious, what else might you forget? Key information in a client's case? It's not a good signal.

Boundaries

Although we have offered some fail-safe concepts for business casual dress, your own sensibilities must come into play, too. Corporate climates vary widely as to what's acceptable. For some, casual means trading a suit for a blazer and tie. For others, it's a sport shirt. For our purposes and for yours, we're going to assume it's never a T-shirt, although even that can be the norm in the tech industry, for example.

Acceptable business casual also varies by region and country. The New Yorker might look fine in a charcoal wool turtleneck under a black-and-white herringbone sports coat with dark trousers. The Hollywood entertainment professional might get away with T-shirt under light V-neck sweater under sports jacket with jeans. The more conventional Midwest and South would see both looks as totally out of place.

It's up to you to assess what fits in. You do that by noting what the highest-ranking males in the office wear on casual days. That's your benchmark. If your colleagues dress much more casually than that, find ways to emulate superiors without looking like a brown-noser. If superiors wear sports coats and dress shirts and your co-workers only wear casual shirts, you wear a casual shirt with sports coat over it. That sort of thing.

Another barometer is how clients dress. You don't want to dress more casually than they do. If your clients consistently wear suits, your authority diminishes if you show up wearing a sport shirt. You'll look off-duty. Even if your office sanctions casual dress, think twice before going along.

It's likely you may view the suggestions here as somewhat restrictive. This is, after all, the twenty-first century. It is common to see fashionably dressed young men with their shirttails out or in a fine sports coat and faded jeans. The problem with this line of thinking in the business world is that most of you will be dealing with men and women of older generations. What you may view as cool they may see as unkempt and unprofessional. Dressing conservatively will never get you in trouble.

There is no need to stress over this, but there is reason for caution: How you dress in casual situations says more about you than your formal business best. Why? Because the dark suit/white shirt/neat tie is easy. What you choose when the formula isn't simple reveals that old attention-to-detail thing again. It's a chance to show off personal savvy—or lack thereof. We're here to help with your homework for an A+ impression.

DEAL KILLER
SPORT SHIRTS WITH DRESS TIES

Silk ties belong with dress shirts. No exceptions. A knit tie can sometimes work with a sport shirt and blazer, provided the shirt is long-sleeved and has a collar that works with a tie. But don't force the issue.

BUSINESS CASUAL

Neatness counts

Remember when you were in kindergarten and your mother tucked your little striped T-shirt into the elastic waist of your color-coordinated shorts because, in her words, neatness counts? Heed her advice as you approach the very grown-up task of dressing for business casual.

Because "casual" can be misinterpreted easily and the clothing can become overly relaxed, keeping your look tidy is essential. Everything must be pressed, clean, and crisp. Always. From the shine on your loafers to the crease in your pants to the starch in your shirt, polish is every bit as important in business casual—perhaps more so.

This is rule No. 1. No exceptions. Make Mom proud.

Quality

Having already stretched your credit limit buying all those essentials for your suit wardrobe, you may be thinking (hoping) business casual won't rack up more finance charges. It even sounds less expensive.

Sorry to disappoint you. Like the impeccable neatness factor, quality is imperative here. It's not that you have to buy the most expensive sports coats, trousers, and shirts for business casual. Rather, you must be careful not to buy the cheapest. In other words, elements of business casual dress are available at modest prices, but they won't create the look you want. Business casual is like shoes in this regard. It's another place many men will be tempted to scrimp. Those who come through with quality get noticed in the right way.

{ Tip: Always—*always*—keep a fresh white dress shirt and classic tie at the office. A dark blazer should be handy, too. If you don't wear one on casual days, keep one at the office. You never know when a client will call or some situation will arise that requires you to be business-presentable at a moment's notice. }

KILLER DEAL
NO ELBOWS

Since a man takes off his jacket at the office, short-sleeved polo shirts are not a good idea for business casual. They're OK for weekend wear, but we're back to that no-bare-arms thing again. Skin is not in, especially in business environments.

Long-sleeved polo knit shirts in cotton, cotton/silk blends, and merino wool are much more acceptable for business casual.

Sweaters

In colder climates, a crewneck wool sweater over sport shirt under blazer or jacket works well for business casual. The sweater keeps you looking more together in the office when the jacket comes off. Stick to solids in colors that won't blind your co-workers.

The collared sweater with two-button placket is another good option—like a long-sleeved polo shirt, only heavier. Again, it looks good in the event you remove your jacket. It is worn over a long-sleeved collared dress or sports shirt and can even be worn with a tie.

The turtleneck and mock turtleneck are option No. 3, but these are far less conservative choices. Although there's a certain sophistication about the turtleneck/blazer look, there's also something clichéd about it. In other words, it can look classic and right or Hollywood cheesy and forced. Much depends on the wearer, the industry, and the part of the country. Enter at your own risk.

KILLER DEAL
BUTTONS AGAIN

Since "casual" usually means ditching the tie, that begs the question: How many top buttons should be unbuttoned? Button the sport shirt all the way to the top, and you risk looking nerdy. Neat, but nerdy. The only exception is if the top button hits low on the throat and the collar lies flat, as is often the case with soft fabrics like silk. Then the top button can be buttoned. Men with long necks should avoid this style, however.

Equally unappealing is unbuttoning the top two buttons. Now you're talking lounge lizard. No matter how much you treasure your chest, this is not the place to show it.

The safest route is to unbutton the topmost button only, leaving the second button closed. We realize this may not create the optimum look with all shirts. Depending on how the shirt is made, some will look too buttoned up this way, others too loose and unstructured.

What can we say? It's an imperfect world. And if you happen to find a shirt that works just right for you, buy multiples.

Accessories

Business casual allows men to move into slightly less formal shoes and belts. Leather accessories don't necessarily have to be black (although they may be). Handsome brown leathers and suede often work well with sports coats and trousers. Belts with some texture, like a woven leather, are acceptable. Elastic belts never are.

Business casual also allows for slightly more substantial shoes and belt, "slightly" being the operative word here. We're not talking Doc Martens and rodeo buckles. We are talking heavier proportions than dress accessories.

For shoes, you can stay with lace-up oxfords—a classic brown suede cap-toe or wing tip is always tasteful—or go with a slip-on, aka loafer. The cordovan or black loafer modeled after the traditional Bass Weejun is another safe choice.

KILLER
DEAL
LOUD PATTERNS

Please do not make the mistake of thinking a patterned sport shirt means just *any* patterned sport shirt. There is a big difference between a subtle blue and red stripe and a blue and red paisley. The color and pattern on a sport shirt should be tastefully subdued. Think of it as a dress shirt on two cups of coffee, not on steroids.

The sole might be thicker and the stitching more pronounced, but your business casual shoe should still have an air of dress about it. The leather should be the kind you polish or a refined suede. This is not the place for boat shoes or driving moccasins.

The more casual shoe also calls for a heavier sock, somewhere between wool hiking socks and thin dress hosiery. A nice, non-transparent flat knit works here, maybe with a hint of texture. Tiny repeating patterns or knitted textures are also acceptable, but not advisable. Argyles are definitely out of the question. You really don't want to draw attention to your ankles.

Caps of any sort—especially baseball—are not part of a professional look, not even a casual one. Knit hats are equally bad. You look like a bank robber. We won't even mention earmuffs. If you must have head gear to ward off the weather, a classic fedora remains the best choice. More casual renditions are available in felt and suede.

Outerwear

Again, there are options here driven by what level of business casual is deemed appropriate. If you adopt the blazer or sports coat approach (which we highly recommend), you need to stick with a tailored overcoat. The full-length coat you wear with suits is fine.

Or, if the budget allows, consider adding a three-quarter length coat. This is sometimes called a "car coat." It resembles the longer overcoat, but may button all the way up to a shortened collar instead of having lapels. Some car coats are zip-front. Wool, twill, and poplin are acceptable fabric choices depending on your need for warmth and/or water repellent. Colors range from black, dark navy, or charcoal to camel to khaki for the poplin. Subtle salt-and-pepper or earthy tweeds are also nice.

If a sport shirt without a sports coat is the accepted business casual look, you can opt for a sportier jacket. By "sportier," we're thinking a nice suede or solid wool jacket for example, not one inspired by your favorite team. Color and cut should be conservative, and it should be long enough to hit mid-thigh (nix the baseball jacket). As with everything, quality is key—especially if it is leather. There's nothing worse than a cheap leather jacket.

We know you may be tempted on frigid business casual Fridays to haul out your down jacket with the big cozy hood or the coveted shearling coat you wear on winter vacation. Unless it's a certified blizzard, resist. Instead, add a beefy crewneck sweater, cashmere scarf, whatever you need to keep warm beneath a more conservative, tailored coat. Jackets worn for recreation retain that impression. You are supposed to be working here.

THE LAST WORD ON BUSINESS CASUAL

Look in the mirror right before you walk out the door in the morning. If anything—*anything*—about your business casual look gives you the slightest pause, change clothes. It's not worth it.

DEAL KILLER CARDIGANS

It may seem perfectly logical that a fine cardigan sweater might take the place of a sports coat for business casual. Logical, but potentially lethal.

Some expensive, heavy-knit, shawl-collared cardigans look quite masculine and cool over sport shirts, but those are grand exceptions.

Sadly, most long cardigans just come off looking frumpy. Stay-at-home-with-the-flu frumpy. It's not a good look.

We all loved Mr. Rogers, but we do not want to emulate his style.

BUSINESS CASUAL WARDROBE

As with elements of the expanded business wardrobe, business casual becomes a matter of increased choice. A man has before him a smorgasbord of color and texture, far more than he encounters with his business wardrobe. Since this section of his closet also serves many of his social occasions, sports coats and blazers are the mainstay. He will tend toward cashmere and camel hair for winter wear, linens and silks for summer, some mixture of fine fibers for transitional months.

He may be the sort of man who prefers to stick to solids in his jackets and express himself with color in shirts and ties. Or he may gravitate toward tasteful colors in tweeds or patterns for his jacket fabrics complemented with quieter shirts.

In any case, business casual offers opportunities to exude personal style and show off quality: for example, pairing the rich texture of a beautiful Harris tweed sports coat over a high-grade cashmere polo with a fine wool gabardine trouser and beautiful leather loafer.

As with the business wardrobe, the best in business casual—specifically jackets, trousers, and cotton shirts—will be custom-made. Knit shirts in fine cottons, silks, wool, or blends will not be. In keeping with the gentleman's wardrobe, fabric and construction will always be the finest available.

SPORTS COATS

1. Navy blazer in a year-round wool
2. Navy blazer—100 percent cashmere or wool flannel
3. Camel or vicuna tan blazer
4. Black blazer—midweight
5. Blue check or plaid
6. Olive check or muted plaid
7. Black-and-white Prince of Wales plaid
8. Black and gray houndstooth check
9. Rich brown muted pattern
10. Summer light tan or blue-gray

TROUSERS

1. Tan wool gabardine
2. Olive wool gabardine
3. Navy wool gabardine
4. Gray flannel
5. Gray worsted wool (summer)
6. Khaki or tan twill or chino
7. Navy worsted wool (summer)
8. Tan worsted wool (summer)
9. Black gabardine
10. Navy linen
11. Black linen
12. Beige linen
13. Textured (like Donegal tweed), navy dominant
14. Textured, black dominant
15. Textured, brown dominant
16. Corduroy

SHIRTS

- 6 assorted cotton sport shirts in dark shades for winter
  The assortment includes some oxford cloth, some broadcloth (Pima, Egyptian, or Sea Island); some spread collar, some button-down; and a mixture of solids and patterns (mini-check, tattersall check, etc.)
- 6 assorted cotton sport shirts in light shades for summer (same variety as winter)
- 6 long-sleeved knit three-button polo shirts
- 6 short-sleeved pique or Sea Island cotton knit polo shirts
- 2 black or navy mock turtlenecks

SWEATERS: For wear primarily beneath a sports coat:

- Neutral cotton V-neck
- Cotton crewneck
- Cashmere knit vest, solid or with pattern
- Navy, yellow, white, brown cashmere polo
- Cashmere crewneck

SHOES

1. Black pebble-grained leather or burnished calf casual lace-up
2. Brown nubuck oxford
3. Black or brown lace-up with Vibram outsole for inclement weather
4. Black lightweight Italian slip-on (Gucci, kiltie, tassel)
5. Burgundy slip-on
6. Brown slip-on

BELTS

1. Black alligator/lizard/other exotic
2. Brown alligator/lizard/other exotic
3. Black woven leather
4. Brown woven leather
5. Black or brown with small silver buckle and silver tip
6. Cordovan, woven or smooth

OUTERWEAR

3/4-length black or taupe microsuede to repel water, zip-in lining

3/4-length camel hair coat

3/4-length black or navy cashmere coat

3/4- or full-length suede coat

Double-breasted full-length tweed coat

Luggage

Luggage can be a many-splendored thing. A beautifully seasoned, sumptuous leather portmanteau speaks to all things masculine, adventure, and romance like few other possessions.

Unfortunately, it also speaks to dishonest baggage handlers and thieves.

Fine luggage serves as a moving billboard for what's inside. Better to be one of the masses this time. Pass up the rich cowhide for a quality, durable case in serviceable black ballistic nylon. Invest in a hanging suit bag on wheels that holds two to three suits and a week's worth of shirts. Mark it as your own with a distinctive, but tasteful, luggage tag. Save the colorful duffles for weekend getaways. They are not business luggage.

Use a structured case or suit bag. If the trip requires more than the hanging suit bag, pack two medium bags rather than one large one. Two bags are more balanced and easier to carry than one big unwieldy one.

Wheels no longer look girly. Use them. Airports can seem like marathons. Porters can be nonexistent. Travel smart.

{ Travel tip: As your wardrobe expands, choose suit fabrics that are comfortable and serviceable. There's nothing worse than being stuck on a cross-country red-eye in pants that itch. Fabrics like nail's head, herringbone, bird's eye, and English tic weave don't show wear, spots and wrinkles like solids. }

{ Another travel tip: Dress up, rather than down, for travel, especially flying. Watch how much better people treat you. }

Professional Advice: Always pack one more shirt than you think you'll need.

Packing sometimes confounds men, but it shouldn't. It's not hard. Think of it as a small-scale engineering project.

- Select a bag that will hold everything snugly. It shouldn't be jammed, but clothes shouldn't be swimming around, either. The less garments shift, the better they arrive.

- Shoes tend to crush things, so put them in the bottom of the bag. Take one pair of cedar shoe trees or at least stuff socks inside shoes to save space and help shoes save shape. Be careful that shoe polish or dirty shoe bottoms don't leave footprints on your important clothes. Use shoe bags (good shoes come with them) or wrap a paper sack or old undershirt around shoes.

- Around the shoes, stuff underwear, pajamas, belts, and anything else that doesn't mind wrinkles. This is a good place for the shaving kit. For double security, put anything that can leak (shampoo, mouthwash, sunscreen, etc.) in sealable plastic bags. The few extra minutes precaution could save your entire wardrobe from disaster.

- Next layer takes sweaters, T-shirts, shorts, knit shirts, and trousers. The less you fold and crease clothes going in, the better they look coming out. Every fold is a wrinkle in the making, so fold gently and sparingly.

- A great trick is to place dress shirts, trousers, and suit jackets on wire hangers (just for shape) and cover individually with plastic dry cleaning bags. Then lay each plastic-covered garment as flat as possible in the bag. Or you can tie the bag at the bottom to create the airbag effect. In either case, the plastic reduces friction against the garment, which in turn reduces wrinkles.

- If you are carrying a hanging suit bag, hang several dress shirts on top of each other on the same hanger. You can even put trousers beneath them and a suit jacket over them so you have to carry only a single hanger. The principle at work here is the less clothes shift around, the less they will wrinkle.

PACKING FOR TWO DAYS OUT OF TOWN ON BUSINESS

The starter wardrobe travels easily, because it's built on basics that coordinate. Even if you have built beyond those basics (congratulations), go back to them for the sake of efficient good looks out of town. Wear a solid dark suit, black belt/socks/dress shoes, white shirt, tie. Pack one pair of trousers that work under your suit jacket in a pinch; two versatile ties; two white shirts, one blue shirt; casual shoes; two pairs of socks; three pairs of underwear; and workout clothes if necessary. Toss in your shaving kit (see Chapter Six for contents), which should remain packed at all times, drape topcoat or raincoat over your arm as needed, grab your briefcase, and you're off.

www.tomjames.com

How you look makes critical first impressions. How you act makes lasting ones.

What we're talking about here is class, a word that is overused and often distorted today.

Class and money do not necessarily go hand in hand, although the man with class is more apt to make money. Class is never presumptuous, arrogant, or showy. Quite the contrary. Simply put, class is knowing how to make everyone else comfortable. *Everyone else.*

In turn, knowing how to make others comfortable makes you comfortable. It's a classic win-win.

Funny how many people don't get it.

The good news is this presents a fine opportunity for distinction. Hence, a chapter with some basics on class.

Knowing the code helps. Some call it "manners" or "etiquette." We prefer to call it "confidence," because that's what we're building. Knowing instinctively which napkin is yours, how to make proper introductions, and what to do at a business dinner all instill confidence. When a client asks you to lunch, you are free to focus on the conversation, not the order of silverware. That's confidence.

Furthermore, like the shine of your shoes and the care of your nails, showing courtesy and good manners demonstrates attention to detail. Those who mind details appear brighter and more trustworthy. That's good business.

There is nothing phony, restrictive, or outdated about any of this. To quote *The Metrosexual Guide to Style,* "…sophistication in its truest sense is not an affectation, but rather an inherent understanding of accepted social behaviors." This is about those accepted social behaviors. Chivalry is dead only if you want your career to be, too. Courtesy and manners exist so you'll know what to do at all times to put yourself and others at ease.

This, my good man, will never go out of style.

Two things happened in the twentieth century that call into question many long-held social customs. One is equality for women, especially in the workplace, and the other is society's movement toward more relaxed rules of acceptable conduct.

Years ago, for example, a mid-level manager would never have presumed to address the company's CEO by his first name. This manager could have also helped a female co-worker with the door without fear of offending her.

> Tip: We hate to be trite, but attitude really is everything. If you cannot be gracious and enthusiastic as you extend yourself in courtesy, don't bother. Holding the door open for someone as you scowl and tap your foot benefits neither party.

The rules are less clear these days. You'll have to rely on your own wits from time to time. Our best advice is to err on the side of caution— i.e., call the boss "Mr." or "Ms." unless he or she instructs otherwise—and treat everyone courteously, not just women. If you wait until all the other people—male and female—get off the elevator before you do, no one will complain.

That said, it is our sense that everyone appreciates consideration, women especially. Courtesies considered sexist in the proving ground of the late twentieth century no longer threaten most women. Opening the car door for her is more apt to be viewed as thoughtful than chauvinistic.

The PC Dilemma

Punctuality

The frantic pace of today's lifestyles taxes even the most organized among us. Being punctual when the world stays chronically overscheduled poses huge challenges.

This is precisely the reason you must be punctual. Without fail. No one has time to wait. You make them wait, you lose face.

Being late goes beyond that, however. Those who say they'll be there at 3:00 and show up at 3:10 are breaking a personal contract. They're going back on their word. Who's to say they can be trusted with more weighty matters? Like business.

Sometimes people keep others waiting as a power play, a way of control. Don't get sucked into that game. Find another place to play where men are more secure and the rules are fair.

Last but not least, being on time demonstrates you are someone on whom others can count. It says you are thoughtful and, once again, details are important.

If circumstances beyond your control make you late to an appointment or meeting, do your best not to interrupt proceedings already under way. Don't come in babbling about bad traffic, gesturing and drawing attention to yourself. Enter quietly, nod a quick apology to the speaker, take a seat as inconspicuously as possible, and save any explanations and verbal apologies until the meeting is over.

If you find yourself unavoidably detained for even five minutes, always call to alert those waiting. To neglect this courtesy compounds the aggravation of waiting with the angst of wondering if the absentee will show up at all. Getting word to your victims shows consideration and softens the offense.

If you are late to a business lunch or other small gathering, a brief but sincere apology upon arrival suffices. Follow with an equally brief explanation if you feel so moved, but avoid laying blame on circumstances, as that appears irresponsible. Definitely do not belabor your transgression with a lengthy explanation, unless your tardiness is the result of alien abduction or some equally fascinating phenomenon.

Follow-up

Today's frenetic pace and on-to-the-next-thing mentality make tidying up yesterday's affairs rare. That is all the more reason why nonessential follow-up distinguishes an individual like little else. Put simply, it makes you unforgettable.

Those who mail resumés and then follow with a note or a call get the interview. Those who follow interviews with a handwritten note thanking the executive for her time get jobs. Those who follow potential client encounters with notes stating "nice to talk with you" get business.

The chain of positives never ends.

Following up speaks to character and attention to detail. It says you care enough to give something thought and time even after the fact. It makes the recipient of this attention feel extra special.

Follow-up can also be about keeping promises and, therefore, integrity and trust. If you say to someone "Let's have lunch sometime" but never call to set that up, you're breaking your word. Sure, everybody does it. That's why those who actually follow through make such an impact.

If you say you're going to do something, do it. If you say, "I'll call you," call. If you tell someone you'll send over the magazine article discussed at the meeting, mail it. If you promise to introduce a client to a friend, set that up. Your stock will rise measurably.

Take this to the next level by following through in a way that lets someone know you were really paying attention. For example, if during lunch your client mentions she collects vintage Jaguars, follow up on the lunch by enclosing your handwritten note in a really good book on the subject. (Note: Research on line to ensure it is a good book; otherwise you'll come off as well-meaning but stupid.)

In most cases, note that we recommend handwritten notes. E-mail is better than nothing, but just barely. Your well-intentioned follow-up is liable to be buried in spam and never read. Besides, writing something by hand denotes time and thought. It's a stunning gesture these days.

Since follow-up is about going the extra distance, this is a good place to mention that acknowledging any of life's peak occasions endears. When congratulations or condolences are in order, be prompt about adding yours. Write a note, send a gift, or, if appropriate, show up. They'll never forget it.

Honesty

Why would we include a word on honesty in this chapter? Because a lack of it seems to be running rampant in today's business world.

Somehow we have gotten the idea it's OK to stretch the truth to suit our purposes. This can be especially tempting as one begins a career. A minor inflation of college extracurriculars on the resumé, a slight fabrication of experience in the interview, a little too carried away with how well you know so-and-so. The next thing we know, Enron or impeachment from office.

Blame it on today's intense competitiveness at every level, but never excuse it. Lies, no matter how little or white, have a way of coming back to bite you.

Being truthful and trustworthy is the most essential part of character. Don't forget it.

body language

BODY

Countless studies on the art of communication have found that human judgment hinges far more on the nonverbal than the verbal. People often decide whether they like us, believe us, trust us, want to listen to us before we ever speak.

This not only underscores everything herein about grooming and dressing; it also emphasizes the importance of posture, facial expression, and gesture. These are not just personal quirks; they're vital communication tools that can work for you or against you. How you stand, where your eyes are focused, and what you do with your hands as you speak can enhance what you say or totally negate it. Hard to believe, but it's true.

Eye contact and handshake are two elements of body language discussed later in the chapter in more depth. Other points for consideration include the following:

LANGUAGE

- **Posture:** You don't have to be tall to have great presence. You do have to have good posture. It's like Mother said: Stand and sit up straight (sit on cheeks and thighs, not tailbone). Place feet squarely on the floor, weight evenly balanced between them. Keep shoulders back and head high over shoulders, not thrust forward. Be careful to look strong, but never rigid. Keep muscles relaxed. Sitting or standing, you'll look inches taller and more commanding.

- **Walk:** How you walk into a room gives others the first signal as to how they feel about you and how you feel about yourself. You should enter with head held high, looking awake, open, ready. There should be no hesitation in your stride, but you need not walk fast. Indeed, the point is not to charge the room. You are not a Hun. Enter respectfully with anticipation. Shoes should emit a distinct "click, click, click" if you're walking properly and with good posture. Excessive scraping indicates shuffling. Avoid that. Walk purposefully. You know, like you're going somewhere.

- **Gestures:** This is where videotaping is especially valuable. Many of us don't realize how (or if) we gesture or what physical habits we might have that distract others. Some people have a subconscious habit of licking their lips. Others may continually adjust eyeglasses or rub their palms together as they speak. Most of the time, we don't notice these things in ourselves, but others do. And they can annoy clients to the extent of avoiding us. Even worse, some gestures, like pointing with the index finger as you talk, can be truly offensive, especially in certain cultures.

- **Nuances:** Volumes are devoted to the finer details of body language and what they mean. If you wish to delve more into it (a good idea for any businessperson), any bookstore or bookselling Web site will oblige. For the sake of example here, however, be aware of a few of the more common and transparent signals to avoid: crossed arms in front of the body as a sign of defensiveness or being close-minded; furrowed brow or silence as disagreement or disapproval; slight smile as not taking the matter seriously; heavy sigh as frustration or contempt; lack of eye contact as lack of interest.

Professionals who learn to use nonverbal signals effectively create personal power and strength. It may take time and practice before these elements feel natural and come across as authentic—essential if they're to have the right impact. The best method is to videotape yourself, and then critique, learn, and improve.

DEAL KILLER KEEP YOUR HANDS TO YOURSELF

Communication through touching is a touchy subject. Many human behaviorists will tell you touching another person can have many positive and powerful connotations. Some professionals use the brief hand on the shoulder like eye contact: to imply connection and make the other person feel important. The hearty pat on the back or nudge with the elbow may be used the same way.

This is a bad idea for many reasons. First, touching is more apt to make someone feel demeaned, because it comes off as fatherly or a senior-to-junior gesture.

Second, many people don't like to be touched—period. Slap them on the back or nudge them with your elbow only if you don't mind being punched in the face, which is what these gestures often make us want to do.

Third, in some cultures, touching violates dignity.

And last, but certainly not least, in today's society those who touch—however well-meaning—are a sexual harassment lawsuit waiting to happen.

CONFIDENCE

HANDSHAKE

If there is a top 10 do's and don'ts of making first impressions, the handshake would be No. 2 on the list after appearance.

Your handshake is your physical signature. It's one of those things that locks into people's memories filed under your name. Pay attention.

Actually, "shake" is something of a misnomer. In today's world, it's more of a grasp with little or no up-and-down motion. Keep it that way.

A good handshake is firm, never limp, never bone-crushing. Simply take another's hand in yours as if you were grasping a substantial doorknob. Don't hesitate. Reach in all the way. The valley between your thumb and forefinger should lock firmly against the same of the hand you shake.

Grip the hand but don't squeeze. Keep your wrist and forearm rigid. Look the other person in the eye as you do this. Hold the hand for about three seconds, or long enough to hear his or her name if you're being introduced and for you to offer your name. A more casual shake might only be a second. Then you can relax your hand and withdraw.

A FEW MORE POINTERS ON AN EFFECTIVE HANDSHAKE:

- Always be the one to initiate a handshake. Don't wait for the other person to gesture. Male or female, it doesn't matter. Stick your hand out.

- Approach the other person squarely, smile, make and hold eye contact, and extend your hand with fingers slightly parted and thumb pointed straight up. Grasp the other hand so the flesh between your thumb and palm locks into the same space on the other person's hand. This assures full grasp, not a timid half-in/half-out approach.

- Hold the hand firmly, but do not squeeze. This is not a testosterone test. Overkill on a handshake is as big a turnoff as the limp fish grip. Too much muscle gives the impression you have something to prove. Besides, if

either person is wearing rings or has arthritis, a crushing handshake can be truly painful. Pump the hand at least once, but no more than three times. Hold it for a count of three, no more than five, before releasing. Don't rush it. Pulling away too quickly can seem either brusque or insecure, but holding too long is creepy.

- For the entire duration of the handshake, maintain eye contact. If you must look at your hand to ensure the connection, do so only momentarily. Better that than have your hand wind up where it shouldn't be.

- Avoid the two-handed handshake unless you know the person well. It denotes a certain intimacy and warmth that may not be appropriate in business situations. It may come across as patronizing or demeaning.

- Similarly, extending the index finger to touch the other person's wrist can seem affected. This is business, not secret fraternity signals.

- Offer the same degree of firmness for both men and women. Many men tend to loosen their handshake for a woman. Don't do this. Women don't like to feel a noodle-y hand any more than men do. If your handshake is as it should be, you're not going to hurt her.

- Also, some men don't feel obliged to shake a woman's hand, especially in social situations. That's a mistake. Unless you're on kissing terms, always offer a woman your hand. It's offensive if you don't.

- If you want to experience a good handshake, ask a confident female to shake hands. Women tend to make a handshake substantial without force. It's a combination of less strength and, more significantly, less need to come across as macho.

DEAL ■ KILLER
SPACE
INVADERS

Everyone knows someone who insists on standing too close during conversation. It's one of those physical offenses that can tube otherwise promising careers. Especially if you are trying to do business among one of several foreign cultures that deem such closeness not merely offensive, but insulting.

America's rules are less rigid, but nonetheless important. Americans don't like to be breathed upon. They like personal space somewhere between three and six feet around them. We all typically like more space between us and those we don't know well, less as the relationship feels familiar.

For purposes of business, maintaining physical distance is essential. If you enter a client's personal space, you make him or her uncomfortable and unwilling to listen to what you have to say.

One clue: If you often begin talking to someone while standing in one part of a room and find by conversation's end, the two of you have moved to another part of the room, it may be because the person you've engaged continues to back away from you.

It's a good sign that you need to back off, buster.

EYE

Shaking hands isn't the only time eye contact is critical. In all circumstances, looking someone in the eyes gives you power.

Think of one of the most boring, least engaging teachers you ever had. Chances are he or she didn't look students in the eye during class very often. The professor didn't connect, so you didn't either.

Or how about this: Have you ever been at a party or lunch with someone and while you were talking, he or she began looking past you at someone else? Is there anything more dismissive, defeating, annoying?

Those who maintain strong eye contact exhibit confidence and elicit trust. It demonstrates focus and indicates listening. There's nothing better.

A word of clarification: Making eye contact does not mean staring like a lunatic. You are not trying to read minds here, nor do you wish to intimidate. Don't lock eyeballs. Look away naturally but briefly, and always come back to the eyes. The idea is to show respect.

CONTACT

SITUATIONS TO NOTE:

- When you come into an office or room to meet someone, resist the natural tendency to look around. Instead, make eye contact with that individual(s) as soon as you enter and then maintain it. Not at the risk of tripping over the furniture, of course, but within reason.

- Since eye contact denotes listening, use it not only in conversation, but also when listening to a speaker and especially in meetings. Minds tend to wander in meetings, as do eyes. Making eye contact with whoever is speaking and nodding appropriately every once in a while keeps you engaged and flatters the speaker. But don't fake it or get overzealous, Mr. Bobblehead. You'll lose all credibility.

- As illustrated by the example of the forgettable teacher, making eye contact with one's audience as a speaker is essential. Everyone remembers a speaker who attached himself or herself to notes on a podium and never looked up. It's dismal. Dynamic speakers look their audience members in the eyes as if the conversation were one-on-one. It's charming and powerful.

CONFIDENCE

One of the most important aspects of personal presence—if not the most important—is one of the least tangible: energy. It is the aspect of self that either commands others' attention to us or causes us to be ignored.

The characteristics of a good handshake can be defined. The characteristics of good energy, however, are far more elusive. But when someone has it, you know it. Conversely, if someone lacks it, you also know it.

Don't confuse energy with being peppy or hyper. These are actually negative forms of energy because being frenetic repels people. Think of the coming-on-too-strong stereotypical salesman or deejay. Negative energy.

To the other extreme, those who slouch in a chair, stare at the floor, speak too slowly, mumble, or show little or no emotion or expression: They, too, give off negative energy.

If we have to pin a definition on good energy, it would be "confidence expressed."

It's giving off a positive sense of self, of involvement, excitement, and spirit—joie de vivre, if you will. Those who possess it may be charged and extroverted or calm and reassuring.

Think of the magnetic actors or athletes you've seen interviewed. These people are typically passionate about what they do, and that passion energizes every aspect of their lives. It has little to do with good looks and resumé, and everything to do with attitude.

How do you get this kind of energy? The simple answer is to be happy and act that way. "Happy" does not necessarily mean satisfied or joyful, in love, and out of debt. It certainly doesn't mean pie-in-the-sky euphoric. That only raises suspicion about your credibility and sanity.

It means you are genuinely interested and engaged in the world around you and able to demonstrate that to others.

How? By attitude. By being at ease with yourself and open to those around you. By being approachable, making eye contact (there it is again), speaking up, being courteous, smiling. By giving others signals you're a player.

The bottom line: Act as if you matter—not arrogantly, of course, but confidently. Be respectful of others, but never intimidated by them. Don't be shy about participating in meetings, conversations, introductions, opportunities. Be assertive without aggression.

If someone asks your name and what you do, don't share the information as if you're apologizing. Don't brag, either, but sound as if you're glad to be where you are, doing what you do, even if you aspire beyond the position.

Indulge us in a brief exercise. Look at yourself in the mirror. Doesn't matter what you have on. Give it your best "I am exhausted, underpaid, and underappreciated" look (we know you have one; everyone does). Watch your face and shoulders droop and your whole body turn inward on itself. Is this someone with whom you want to do business, dinner, anything?

Now, try on "I just got a huge raise, a new Porsche, and a date with the Luscious twins." Look again. What do you see? Someone dynamic, intriguing, and magnetic. The only thing changed was attitude.

Remember this as you go into the world. People gravitate toward good energy. Even better, they find it contagious.

DEAL KILLER
JUDGE NOT

As valuable as it is to understand the impact of our own nonverbal communication, there is another equally important lesson here. That is how quickly we humans draw conclusions from often insignificant cues. Or, as the old saying goes, "to assume is to make an 'ass' out of 'u' and 'me.'"

Assuming a colleague slumped in his chair with eyes lowered during a meeting isn't paying attention misses the fact he is quietly solving the problem. Pegging someone as cold and intimidating who is really just shy may dismiss a potentially valuable relationship. Thinking someone who keeps her arms crossed isn't open to new ideas could keep you from finding the perfect backer for your product. She may just be cold.

In other words, work to project the proper nonverbal signals yourself, but don't be so quick to judge others on this basis. Such assumptions will, in all likelihood, shortcut some of life's great opportunities.

VOICE QUALITY

Whether you are speaking to one, twenty-one or 10,001, voice makes a difference. The tone, pitch, volume, and speed of delivery either make people want to listen, or not. Not all of us can sound like James Earl Jones or Sean Connery. Thank goodness. It would make the world an audibly boring place.

We can all maximize the instrument we've been given to make sure we are communicating effectively and optimally.

WHAT TO CONSIDER:

• Breathing properly is essential. Breathing properly supports the voice; lends volume, clarity, and depth; regulates cadence; and calms us down. When we become anxious, our first response is to hold our breath. It has done in many a public speaker. A good exercise is to lie flat on the floor and place one palm flat over your navel. Relax and breathe deeply until you feel your breath becoming regular and your stomach area rising as you inhale, falling as you exhale. This is proper breathing, using the diaphragm. Practice this until you are able to breathe this way on cue. It will work wonders for your voice and overcome nerves. Remembering to breathe deeply will allow you to be dynamic in all circumstances.

• Talking fast may be symptomatic of today's society, but it's not good business. If you find you're often repeating yourself in order to be understood, try slowing down. Take a breath after every sentence for pacing. Put distinct endings on your words, like "ing." Pronunciation forces you to slow down, and it's like Mom said: "Don't mumble."

• To improve the quality of your voice on the phone, smile as you talk. This sounds silly, but it works. Smiling lifts the spirits and makes the voice friendlier and more energetic.

Tip: If any of the skills outlined in this chapter—maintaining eye contact, handshake, posture, making introductions, etc.—makes you uncomfortable, practice, practice, practice. Otherwise, your actions will seem forced and false and have the direct opposite effect of what you intend.

Business Soc

Business cards

Like a clean handkerchief and underwear, you should never leave the house without business cards. You never know when you'll need one. Hand them out liberally, but not obnoxiously. Let others know you are ready to be of service.

Better still, ask others for their business cards. It's a subtle form of interest and flattery. At the first possible opportunity, pen a few notes on the back about where you met the person, what you discussed, anything else pertinent. File those cards in a binder designed for that very purpose.

Then if you really want to blow someone away, drop him or her a handwritten (not e-mail) "nice talking with you" note following up or use the information to write a personal line on a holiday card. In these days when we endure so much that is impersonal, such attention is unforgettable.

Name tags

Name tags always go on the right breast or lapel so the person shaking your hand is looking directly at your name.

If it is a "do-it-yourself" name tag, print clearly and large enough so the far-sighted entrepreneur with millions to invest with you can read it. Teeny-tiny handwriting on name tags not only aggravates others; it looks as if you are not fully present and/or friendly.

If your handwriting is really that awful, practice at home with a Magic Marker until you grow up.

INTRODUC

DEAL KILLER
AND YOU ARE…?

Through ignorance, arrogance, or an unfortunate case of social nerves, people sometimes fail to introduce themselves. This is especially flagrant when another person introduces himself or herself to you and you do not reciprocate.

To wit: *Tyler Stein approaches Mr. Doofus. "Hello, I'm Tyler Stein." Tyler sticks out his hand to shake Mr. Doofus's hand. Mr. Doofus takes Tyler's hand, shakes it, smiles cordially, and says, "Nice to meet you, Tyler." Period.*

Always, always be quick to state your own name. Not only is this Manners 101, it saves embarrassing situations. Sometimes a person introducing you to a third party may not be able to recall or pronounce your name. Sometimes a person introduces himself or herself to you as a way to get you to restate your name.

Never assume others know your name. Regardless of how important you think you are, humility is always the true sign of class.

Protocol for making introductions used to be strictly defined. You always addressed the highest ranking, oldest person, or female first, then the name of those of lesser rank, age, or gender (just kidding).

This order stems from days of yore when visitors were presented to royalty. One would always address the king and/or queen first, saying, "Your Highness," and then "May I present Prince Charming," or "Larry, Curly and Moe," or whatever plebeians you had dragged before their majesties.

These days, the aforementioned rules are always acceptable and, in certain situations, advisable. But no one is going to cut off your head if you trip up on this. What is essential is to be proactive and quick with introductions. Don't wait for others to make the move. Distinguish yourself by being the catalyst that makes others feel included and puts them at ease.

In the meantime, if you can remember a few courteous rules, even better.

Order

Following ancient protocol, name the oldest person first. *"Mr. Gray, this is Yolanda Young."* This applies if the age difference is obvious—at least twenty to twenty-five years. (Inquire about a person's age only if you wish to tube your career and social life in one fell swoop.)

That same protocol dictates you introduce a man to a woman. *"Yolanda, this is Fred Fresh. Fred, Yolanda Young."* These days, this rule is more flexible, provided both people are near the same age and not distinguished or senior citizens.

Names and titles

When making business introductions, state both first and last names, unless one party is obviously older or particularly distinguished. Examples of when you should omit first names for more formal address:

• Use "Mr." or "Ms." and the last name for those who are elders in the company and/or community and/or most people address them by last name.

• Use official titles like "Senator," "Doctor," "Reverend," "Father," "Colonel" with the person's last name, but do not use company titles like "president" or "vice president." This is pretentious and inappropriate. If company status needs to be revealed, after the introduction add, "Mr. Meanee is president of our company."

• When introducing children, teens, or young adults to business associates, always address the adult by Mr., Ms., Mrs., or appropriate title and last name. *"Mr. Schmoe, this is my daughter, Morgan."* If the child's last name is different from your own, include that. Let Mr. Schmoe say, *"Please, call me Joe"* if he feels that way. But never introduce an adult by first name to a young person.

If it's a first meeting, shake someone's hand when you meet and when you depart. As you part, always say, "Nice to meet (or see) you." Do this even if it has been hours since you were introduced.

People's names are important to them, so one of the more serious gaffes is to call someone by the wrong name. But, inevitably, it happens to all of us. If you are the transgressor, apologize sincerely the moment you realize your error, even if it is much after the fact. The next time you see the person, go out of your way to call him or her by the correct name, acknowledge your fault, and apologize.

If you are called by the wrong name, whether or not you correct it is up to you. But if the relationship is important and bound to go forward, you do the person a favor by making a gentle correction the first time he or she errs. If he calls you Tom, you simply say, "Sorry, it's Bob." When he apologizes, tell him not to worry because you are often confused with your older brother, partner, or, best yet, some fabulously irresistible movie star with that name. Humor is always the best defuser for awkward moments.

DO YOUR HOMEWORK

There will be times, of course, when the burden of talking will fall to you or when asserting more personality will be to your advantage. The following offers some tips for those times, some do's and don'ts to get things started and, hopefully, keep them rolling:

- Stay informed. Busy schedules may not afford time to read newspapers cover to cover, but there are other ways to keep up. All reasonably sized papers have Web sites where you can find headlines and highlights. Subscribe to a weekly news magazine like *Time* or *Newsweek* and make time to read it. Pick up *The Wall Street Journal* or *New York Times* for business information. Listen to National Public Radio in the morning or afternoon for features, depth, and perspective on stories. Tune into CNN or local news at some point during the day.

- Spend leisure time reading instead of watching trash TV. You will be amazed at how fiction and nonfiction will constantly enhance your conversations. The fact you read also makes you appear thoughtful, smart, and distinguished, provided you don't make it a point to flaunt the pastime.

- If the gathering revolves around business or a company, invest five minutes on line to learn something about that industry, company, etc. This provides talking points for questions only; do not use this to try to impress others with how much you know. Such pretense inevitably backfires.

THE MAGIC BOOK

With so many encounters daily, we often have difficulty remembering what was said in conversations. Remedy this by keeping a journal in your desk and/or at home. Spend a few minutes each day jotting down a note with name and what you talked about. Be specific. The next time you see that person, you can inquire how his or her son's soccer game came out. Nothing scores more points than making others feel you were really paying attention.

Actors working improvisational comedy learn to keep a skit alive by always going along with flow no matter how ridiculous it gets. They have to keep tossing the action to other characters. Once a character either refuses to pick up another character's toss or fails to pass it along, the skit dies.

Opening and moving conversation works in similar fashion. Conversation is about opening topics and keeping them moving forward. You do that by being agreeable, choosing words that invite response, and constantly deflecting attention away from yourself.

Think of times when you've been around someone who dominates conversation. Although part of you may be grateful for the respite in such company, chances are the overall impression isn't favorable. These people come off as self-centered, impolite, and even arrogant. They don't make us feel included and worthy of attention. They don't converse, they lecture. They, in fact, stop conversation.

By contrast, the good conversationalist draws others in and out. He or she keeps his remarks brief and shines the spotlight on others.

This is best done with questions—not prying, personal questions, but gentle, general questions. Start with a statement, on which a bystander can offer opinion/support. Example, "Fifty years in business is quite a milestone, and they've put on a fine reception to celebrate, don't you think?"

If you don't know the person beyond his or her name (*of course* you know the name because you *did* introduce yourself immediately, *didn't you?*), then you might ask if he or she is affiliated with the company. Provided you're not talking to a ficus tree, you will then get information about this person's job and can begin to ask questions that stem from the information you're being given. Again, listening is the key.

If you feel it's not appropriate for conversation to revolve around business and who does what, ask the person if he or she is a sports fan (if you are). Then, *"What teams do you follow?* and so on. Or, a less confining question might be, *"What keeps you busy when you're not working? Any hobbies?"*

Family is usually a safe topic, provided there are no singles or distraught infertile couples in the mix. Weekend activities (*"What are you planning for the weekend?"*) is a good opener among colleagues. This also may give you insight into interests for future conversations.

In situations where time allows for more in-depth conversations, like over lunch or dinner, always come equipped with open-ended questions. A few benign examples:

- "What was your first job?"
- "Where did you grow up?"
- "What brought you to this city?"
- "How did you get interested in (law, medicine, writing, scuba diving, etc.)?"
- "How did you and your wife/husband meet?" (where applicable and if the conversation has turned to personal matters)
- "Where do you like to vacation?"

Getting out of a conversation is every bit as delicate—and maybe even more important—as getting into it. You want to leave people feeling positive, not as if you have abandoned them because they were dull and unwashed. When social conversation has run its course (you'll know), be quick to save everyone from awkward silence by saying, *"It's great to see you (meet you, talk with you). I hope to see you again soon. Enjoy the (party, evening, meeting, etc.)."* You can also use, *"Excuse me, I'm going to freshen my drink (check out the buffet, the view, whatever). It was so nice talking with you."*

CONVERSATION

Conversation closers and killers are two entirely different things. The first category brings an exchange to a pleasant conclusion, the second smothers it.

Following are several common bombs that kill conversation, along with deals and relationships.

- Don't talk about things you know nothing about. This sounds no-brainer, but it's amazing how many people wade into these murky waters. We think if we're not talking, others will think we're stupid. Which begs the question: How does stupid talking help? If the conversation gets over your head or out of your realm, remain quiet and listen with interest. Then ask questions. Being eager to learn is a true sign of intelligence.

- Avoid subjects that are divisive or spark controversy. Politics, religion, certain issues in the news, gun control, abortion, gay marriage, etc. If someone asks your opinion on a hot topic, be diplomatic and, if possible, noncommittal: "I'm not certain of all the facts, so I don't have a firm opinion yet." Be brief and ask quickly, "What are your thoughts about this?" Remain neutral.

- Don't burden business acquaintances with difficult stories. This is not the place to discuss your messy divorce or a big downturn in the market. Your mission with business social conversation is to create an upbeat atmosphere.

- Avoid any references to sex, no matter how benign. It's inappropriate and can really embarrass others.

- Don't complain. You don't have to be Mr. Nauseatingly Happy, but you can be a realist with a glass-half-full perspective. Remember, attitude is everything.

DEAL KILLER
NO $#*!

Profanity, long considered common in the figurative sense, has become common in the literal sense. This proliferation's numbing effect renders previously taboo words less shocking and, to some, less offensive.

But just because a four-letter word is uttered every few seconds on cable, in the movies, and in the halls of high schools doesn't make it appropriate. Some still find profanity—not to mention vulgarity—highly inappropriate. Such language in business settings is like the third cocktail: Don't indulge even if those around you are. It is never becoming, and you don't know whom you might offend.

Remember this: Profanity remains the language of the commoner—those whose limited imaginations cannot yield a more enlightened word or phrase at any given moment. It identifies a man with the uneducated and uncultured masses when distinction is the goal.

- Never tell an offensive joke in a business situation. What's offensive? Just about everything these days. If the joke uses nationality, sex, race, age, hair color, handicap, profession, religion, or family for its punch line, someone might be offended. Don't get lured into thinking it's OK because others at the table have told off-color jokes and chiming in will make you "part of the gang." What you don't know is how others at the table may have felt about the jokes, but aren't saying. We're back to the old adage, "When in doubt, don't." The safest humor is self-effacing. That's always good.

- Don't talk too much. Sometimes we talk and people are laughing and responding and suddenly we think we're Jerry Seinfeld on a roll. Even if you happen to be blessed with the entertainment gene, others still want a chance to talk. Learn to shut up and listen.

- Don't brag. About anything. In fact, downplay those things about yourself you consider impressive. Example: You think you're hot stuff because you were just asked to join a nonprofit board. You want Ms. Big Shot Client to know this so you manage to bring it up during a meeting. What you don't know is Ms. Client has just given an entire wing to the local hospital. She doesn't rub it in, but you look like a lightweight fool. Keep accomplishments and honors to yourself.

- Never discuss income, yours or anyone else's. It's crass and uncomfortable.

- No name-dropping to make yourself appear important. It usually has the exact opposite effect. Besides, you never know who knows whom well and what unfortunate relationships you may be bumping into. If you are genuinely associated with important names that would impress

KILLER
DEAL
TALKUS
INTERRUPTUS

Somewhere among The Top Ten of Rude is the Interrupter, the person who just can't wait until you finish speaking to offer his or her two cents.

Often times, the Interrupter doesn't even understand the offense. Sometimes he or she steps on others' speech out of sheer enthusiasm or wanting to support and agree with what's being said.

Do not think for a moment the speaker appreciates this.

Always allow the other person to finish, completely and totally. Always. Regardless of how boring, long-winded, or misguided another person is, don't interrupt.

Occasionally, there are instances when essential points must be made while another is speaking. If you must interrupt, start with "Excuse me, Dick," say what you must in as few words as possible, then end with, "Dick, please continue."

If you get into a situation where you cannot abide another's ceaseless droning, employ the art of gentle redirection. That is, wait until there is a pause (for breathing, if nothing else), repeat something the person was saying so he or she will know you're listening, and then change the subject. Example, "Tom, that's fascinating about your visit to the pineapple groves in Hawaii, which reminds me that Margaret just returned from another prickly trip—our company's annual meeting. Margaret, please give us the highlights."

DO THE RIGHT THING

There will come a time in conversation (and life) when you either do the right thing or the wrong thing.

If you do the right thing in a big way, someone is liable to compliment or congratulate you. Oddly enough, this makes many of us uncomfortable, and we respond awkwardly. Get over that.

When you receive a compliment, do not insult yourself or the giver by diminishing that for which you're being complimented. (*"Oh, this old tie? My ex-wife gave it to me as a joke."*) It devalues the giver's opinion and rebukes the kindness.

Nor should you reply with, *"I didn't do anything really to deserve the honor."* That's fishing for more compliments and is equally inappropriate.

Instead, say *"Thank you."* Just like Mom taught you. If you like, you may follow with a line that reinforces the compliment, but be careful to remain humble. Examples: *"I love this tie, too."* Or, *"I was truly surprised and honored to be chosen."*

In the latter circumstance—when you do the wrong thing—you must be equally facile with an apology. It is essential to maintaining both character and vital relationships.

But eating crow graciously is far more difficult than accepting a compliment. Apologies require real courage. Prone to make excuses and dodge responsibility, we will go to great lengths to save face amid transgression when all that is required is a simple and sincere, *"I made a mistake. I am sorry."* Overapologizing embarrasses everyone involved, and lengthy explanations dilute the apology. If the sin was committed publicly, the apology should be delivered likewise.

The man who apologizes when he is wrong is a man destined for greater things. Never underestimate that.

THINK BEFORE YOU SPEAK

This can be difficult in times of stress, but it always serves you and others.

To do this, you must learn to be comfortable with a moment of silence around others. Most of us aren't. We feel the need to fill silent voids with conversation. Sitting quietly in an interview is a technique reporters use to get reluctant witnesses to spill the beans. Ditto for salesmen trying to get potential clients to agree to terms.

If you can resist the need for noise, you will have a moment to collect your thoughts before you open your mouth. That moment could save your career.

DEAL KILLER: TALKING TRASH

When we hear gossip or are privileged to private information, our temptation is to pass it along. Why? Because it makes us feel like insiders, it grabs others' attention, it's human nature.

The same applies to negatively critical remarks. Somehow we've come to equate being critical with being smart, clever, sophisticated. We love to tear down and dish dirt.

Muster every last bit of resolve you have and resist these urges. While your listeners may reward you with rapt attention and even encourage more indiscretion, they are also making mental notes. Those notes say, "If he shares this about someone else, wonder what he shares about me?" Their trust and your integrity erode.

You also never know who will tell whom, citing you as the source. Nor can you be positive the people you tell are not in some way affected. How many of you have made a flip remark about someone, only to find out the person you told was married to/in business with/related to/best friends with the object of your scorn?

Suffice to say, gossip is nasty, nasty business. As Shakespeare once said, "Discretion is the better part of valor." That may be out of context, but it still applies.

Whether you are host or guest, there are customs and courtesies to mind when sharing a meal with business contacts. Much of this pertains to social dining as well, so pay close attention. We will not repeat it in Chapter Five. We will, however, go over hosting in one's home in that chapter. Here, we concentrate on dining out.

The Exe

BEFORE

- Choose restaurants that take reservations, if at all possible. Otherwise, there could be a long wait for busy people, which can reflect badly on you.

- Pick restaurants where the noise level won't be such that you can't hold a conversation in a quiet tone of voice. Avoid places where children or other distractions may be.

- Arrive on time. If you are hosting, arrive ten minutes early to make sure you have a good table and the right number of seats.

- Tables near the door, kitchen, or restroom are bad choices. If you are hosting, sit down at the table by yourself for a moment and look around. Is the sun in your eyes from a window? Is it too noisy? Are you too close to other tables for comfortable conversation? Is air-conditioning blowing right on you? If any of these apply, ask to be moved.

- Round tables are preferable for a group. The dynamic gives everyone equal visibility and interaction. Otherwise, some can get stranded outside the group and one-on-one conversations tend to erupt.

- Wait in the foyer for at least one guest to arrive; then be seated. Stand and greet each guest as he or she arrives. If you are host, make introductions. If you are guest, be prepared to stand and introduce yourself as each guest arrives.

- Should you arrive late (you called, of course), offer a brief apology to the group; then walk around the table introducing yourself to everyone you don't know and speaking to those you do. Shake hands with each. Insist they do not get up from their seats. Do not just sit down and let others wonder who you are.

- Place any gear (umbrella, briefcase, etc.) beside your chair beneath the table out of everyone's way. Even better, check these things if that's safe. No cell phones on the table, not even if they're turned off.

- When all guests have arrived, turn off your cell phone, beeper, etc., unless there are medical emergencies pending.

DURING

- Upon sitting down, immediately place your napkin in your lap. It is always the one on your **left**.
- Your water glass and all other glassware are on your **right**.
- Your bread plate is on your **left**.
- Just remember: "Eat to the left; drink to the right." It won't fail you.
- Silverware is used starting from the outside inward toward the plate. If you have three forks, the first would be for the appetizer, the next for salad, the closest for entrée. Dessert forks and spoons are placed at the head of the plate.
- Always greet the waiter in a friendly way. Never be condescending or rude. Say "please" and "thank you" as if you were talking to your mother.
- Beverages will be ordered first and arrive first. It is fine to start partaking when everyone has been served a drink. Sip politely. Do not gulp or slurp. Do not chew ice.
- Don't place a piece of bread directly on the table. If you have no bread plate, wait until your food comes before getting bread.
- Break off a small piece of bread, butter it, and eat it. Don't butter or bite the whole piece of bread at once.
- Indicate you are ready to order by closing your menu. The waiter will pick up on this.
- Be thoughtful about what you order. Drippy soups, stringy pastas, creamy salad dressings, and messy sandwiches can be difficult and unbecoming to eat. Skip the lobster and anything else liable to fling and cling. Stick with dishes that can be eaten easily and cleanly with a fork.
- If the bread basket is in front of you and you have a bread plate, pass the bread. Ditto for sugar, cream, butter. You may take a piece before you pass, but it's nicer if you don't.
- When food begins arriving, wait until everyone at the table is served before you take a bite. When the host or hostess begins to eat, then you may start.
- If you are the only one with a salad or appetizer, inquire if anyone else is waiting for food before beginning.

WHEN YOU ARE FINISHED WITH A COURSE, INDICATE THIS BY PLACING KNIFE AND FORK SIDE BY SIDE LIKE BEDFELLOWS AT 5 O'CLOCK IF YOUR PLATE WERE THE FACE OF A CLOCK.

- If food is too hot to eat, wait. Don't blow on it.
- Never place a used utensil on the tablecloth. Once you use a knife, rest it at an angle on the lip of the bread, salad, or dinner plate—wherever it is being used.
- Never dip a used utensil into community food. For example, don't use the knife with which you've buttered your bread and taken bites to get more butter. Either forgo more butter or ask the waiter for another knife, please. If there is dipping oil, dip only bread you have not touched to your lips.
- Besides bread, do not pick up food with your fingers.
- Eat slowly, taking small bites. You never know when you might be asked a question and need to speak. Cut food into small, manageable bites and eat each bite as you cut it (i.e., don't cut up the whole steak, then eat). Put your silverware down occasionally. This will help slow down eating.
- If someone speaks to you while your mouth is full, smile apologetically, finish chewing, wipe your mouth with your napkin if helpful, and then speak.
- Cut food by switching the knife to your dominant hand and holding the fork in the other. Hold the fork face down to secure the food, then cut. You may either take bits like this (with fork face down) or put the knife down and switch the fork to the dominant hand. Either is fine.
- Wipe your mouth with your napkin frequently, whether you think you need to or not. Never wipe it with anything else, like a hand or sleeve. Also, do not wipe your hands on anything but your napkin.
- If you have to get up from the table before the meal is finished, put your napkin in your seat, not on the table. Napkins go on the table only at the end of the meal.

{ Ordering Tip: If others at the table order appetizers, pre-meal salads, or dessert, do likewise. This saves members of your party from eating alone, something no one likes to do. }

Eat to the left, drink to the right.

TABLE MANNERS

If a friend or associate comes up to the table to greet you during the meal, quickly stand up and shake hands. If you are dining with fewer than four people, introduce each by name. If yours is a large group, introduce the kind intruder by name and say something general about your companions like, *"These gentlemen are visiting us from Mars for a few days to discuss some business. Gentlemen, meet my friend Spock."* Then cut it short and hope the friend/associate/Vulcan moves on quickly.

Although it is no longer essential that a man stand and help a woman with her chair whenever she joins the table, it is the mark of exceptional attention and courtesy.

ORDERING WINE

If you are hosting dinner for associates or clients, it is your responsibility to order wine for the table. This applies only to dinner, as wine is not expected at lunch unless you are in a foreign country that embraces this tradition or are celebrating something special.

If you know there is someone in your party who is extremely knowledgeable about wine, you may ask if he or she would like to order for the table. But be prepared to pay a hefty tab. Also be prepared for him or her to defer back to you.

As a rule of thumb, white wines go with white entrées (chicken, fish) and red wines pair with darker entrées (beef, lamb, pork, pasta). The nicest approach is to order both a bottle of red and a bottle of white. Many like to start with a white and then move to red, depending on their entrée choices.

You do not have to be a connoisseur to pull this off, nor do you have to affect an accent or go to the most expensive wines. It is perfectly acceptable to enlist the help of the restaurant's sommelier (keeper of the wines) or server. If the establishment serves wine, the wait staff should be familiar with the wine list and able to make recommendations. The wine list will be divided into whites, reds, sparkling (Champagne), and sometimes by origin. Simply open the list and say to the sommelier or waiter, *"I would like to order a red and a white. I'm thinking something like this* (pointing to a wine on the list in your price range). *What would you recommend?"*

Or, if you would like to go it alone, get acquainted with a few varieties of wine. Know that most wines are named for a particular grape. Don't get distracted by vintage. That is for the far more educated. For now, variety and price should give you enough ammunition to order an appropriate bottle.

When you find wines you really like, make a note of the grape, the maker, and the year it was produced, along with what you ate, if it was a good match. Save this information somewhere you can reference easily. It's the easiest way to start educating yourself on what to order in the future.

Presentation

Once you have ordered the wine, the sommelier or waiter will bring the bottle(s) to the table and show you the label to verify this is what you ordered. Look at it and nod approvingly, assuming it is correct (which it almost always is).

The wine will be opened table-side and the cork put in front of you. If you desire, sniff the cork to determine if the wine is sour.

A small amount of the wine will be poured into your glass first for tasting. This is not so you can decide whether or not you like it; it's for you to determine if the wine is in suitable condition for drinking. Some wine goes bad during storage for a variety of reasons. It's rare, but it happens.

Take the sampling glass, give it a brief sniff and then take one sip quietly. If it smells really strong (you'll know) or tastes like vinegar or some other foreign substance, ask the server to sample it. Since his or her tip is at stake here, you can bank on getting an honest assessment and quick replacement if the wine is bad. Sometimes a wine will just need to "breathe" for a short time before drinking. Some wines, reds especially, need air for the flavor to improve. Be patient before tasting.

You may also swirl the wine in the glass a time or two. You do this by pinching the stem of the glass between your thumb and your middle and index fingers (the correct way to hold a wine glass). Then gently move your hand in a tiny concentric circle so the wine swirls a bit. Do this before taking that first sip, as swirling can improve flavor. But don't get carried away. The last thing you want is everyone watching as you slosh a nice Cabernet all over yourself and the white tablecloth.

After you take that one sip and find the wine suitable for drinking, nod to the server or say something like, *"Very nice"* or *"That's fine."* The server will then pour for the rest of your guests.

If the server leaves the bottle on the table, a good host keeps an eye on others' wine glasses and offers refills as glasses empty. Pour for those seated on either side of you, and offer to pass the bottle to those whose glasses you cannot reach. It is not necessary that you get up to pour. That is the server's duty. Of course, a really good server will not let a guest's glass become empty, but you can't always count on that.

KILLER DEAL
NO-MARTINI LUNCH

It used to be the "three-martini lunch" marked those in the throes of success. Now it marks those in need of rehab.

If you're smart, you will decline alcohol at lunch, even if everyone else is drinking. These days, a midday nip appears irresponsible at best, or as if you have a real problem, at worst. Neither is good business.

The only exception is joining a Champagne toast initiated by others in special celebration of a deal closing or some such milestone. In this case, a polite sip or two will do. Don't drink half the bottle.

If you are ever in the position to initiate such a toast, do not insist everyone join in. The reasons some people avoid alcohol are always good reasons. Leave them alone.

CONFIDENCE

BUSINESS CLASS

Some of the more common wines follow:

- Cabernet Sauvignon (*"cab-ur-nay sew-vee-nyawn"*) hails primarily from California, but is also the main grape used in French Bordeaux. It is bold and rich. Good with beef.

- Merlot (*"mur-low"*) is a grape related to Cabernet Sauvignon and is often blended with Cabernet Sauvignon. It is dry, richly flavorful, and smooth.

- Pinot Noir (*"pee-no nwahr"*) comes mostly from France and the U.S. It is more acidic than Merlot or Cabernet, and the grape is harder to grow. But it can be magnificent and is versatile for pairing with food, even seafood.

- Zinfandel (*"zen-fen-dell"*) comes from California. Don't confuse this with White Zinfandel, which is an inexpensive sweet blush (pink) wine. A good red Zinfandel tastes robust and fruity.

- Syrah (*"seerah"*) is a full-bodied red that hails from France or Australia. The Aussies call it Shiraz (*"sheer-oz"*). With intense color and slightly sweeter flavor, this wine is particularly good with duck and game

REDS

WHITES

- Chardonnay (*pronounced "shar-donnay"*) is mostly American in origin with bold flavor.
- Pinot Grigio (*"pee-no gree-gee-oh"*) or Pinot Gris (*"gree"*) in French comes primarily from Italy with light and summery flavor. Nice with salads.
- Sauvignon Blanc (*"sew-vee-nyawn blahnk"*) comes mostly from France and California. It can be either crisp and lively or mellow, but is less bold than Chardonnay.
- Gewürztraminer (*"guh-vertz-trah-meaner"*) and Riesling (*"ree-sling"*) are both primarily German wines. These are the sweet wines on the list and, although they can be wonderful, may not suit everyone's taste.

AFTER

- If you are the host or wish to pay the bill without a tug-of-war, excuse yourself before the meal is over and quietly give the waiter your credit card away from the table. It puts others at ease and is a very classy thing to do.

- If the bill is meant to be shared, do not go through who ate what. That's petty. Suggest the bill be divided evenly by the number of people there. Don't forget to add the tip to each portion.

- Always carry two credit cards, one of which is used only for emergencies (i.e., is not approaching its limit). Few things are more embarrassing than having your card denied.

- No toothpicks except in the privacy of a restroom or home alone. If something is stuck in your teeth, never try to dislodge it in public with fingers or anything else. Excuse yourself to the restroom.

- Carry $20 in small bills for tips to valet parkers, cabs, etc., after the meal.

LIFE SAVER

It is destiny that you will find yourself, at one time or another, with an inedible object in your mouth in public. A nasty piece of shell, a gristly bit of meat, an olive pit.

Those elements one is never supposed to swallow, like olive pits, can be slipped gracefully with help from your tongue onto a fork pressed against your lower lip—never spat—then placed on the edge of your plate.

If the offender was never intended to be seen again, like tough meat, discreetly take your napkin, press it to your lips as if wiping your mouth, and slip it into the napkin. Fold the napkin to conceal the object and place it back in your lap. At the first opportunity, quietly ask the waiter for a new napkin.

An important aside: If you swallow something and begin seriously choking, do not get up and go to the men's room. As embarrassed as you may feel sitting there, don't remove yourself from potential lifesaving help. Most deaths from choking occur in the restroom where the victim dies alone. If you see someone who is choking head for the restroom, follow.

DEAL KILLER
EATING DISORDERS

If some people watched themselves eat, it is hard to believe they would continue to do so in the same disgusting fashion.

That is why we suggest you sit down with a plate of a favorite dish, bread, salad, and dessert and a mirror. Watch. Pretend someone is across the table. Talk to him.

What do you see?

Do your lips part when you chew—even slightly, ever? Does your mouth bulge with big bites? Is there food clinging to your lips, mouth, or chin?

Do you want people to avoid dining and socializing with you at all costs?

None of these things should stare back in your reflection. The only time your lips should part is to insert a small bite. Even then, it shouldn't be a gaping orifice. Chewing should be slow and barely discernable.

While you're at it, listen. Do you make any noise when drinking, eating soup, or chewing? Do your lips smack or teeth click against the silverware? Do you sound like a Dirt Devil vacuum when sipping coffee?

Don't laugh. This is not funny.

It's the stuff that makes people avoid you. Even if you have a billion dollars and a hot wife, people will notice and remember your horrid table manners.

Practice good habits until they are instinctive.

CONFIDENCE

Et cetera

Tipping

The standard tip is between 15 and 20 percent of the bill in restaurants. Always verbally thank the people you tip. To simply leave money is not sufficient. Speaking of which, tipping should always be discreet. But do be generous. Magnanimous gestures are their own reward.

- **Maître d':** $5-$20—the minimum for basic service, the maximum for a great table on a crowded evening in a choice restaurant.
- **Bartender:** $1 per drink, alcoholic or soda
- **Washroom attendant:** $1
- **Valet parker:** $2 minimum, $5 in more metropolitan cities. If it's pouring down rain and the poor chap has to sprint five blocks to retrieve your BMW, be extra generous.
- **Coat check:** $1 per item checked or $2, whichever is greater
- **Cab driver:** Between 10 to 15 percent of the fare if he or she didn't take you for a ride, more if the driver gave you great information on the city or was just particularly charming. If the cab is dirty, the driving unnerving, or the driver rude, don't feel obliged to tip.

- **Skycap:** $1 per bag (plus an extra $20 if he saves you from missing your flight).
- **Bellman:** If the bellman takes your bags to your room, the tip should be at least $5.
- **Doorman:** $1-$5 handling luggage, depending on how many pieces; $1 for getting a cab; $5 if it's raining/snowing/cold and cabs are at a premium.
- **Concierge:** depends on services rendered. If she gets you reservations at the hottest restaurant in town, great tickets to a sold-out show, and arranges transportation, at least $20. Come down commensurate with level and difficulty of service.

Holding doors

If a door opens in front of you—elevator, bus, store, office, etc.—let people exit before you enter. Sometimes people will hesitate before exiting, hold the door open, and gesture for you to come in first. In that case, it is acceptable to enter if, and only if, you offer an audible and gracious "thank you."

If you approach a door with one or more people—male or female—open the door and stand while everyone else enters. If it happens to be a revolving door, be the last to enter—and never with another person in the same partition.

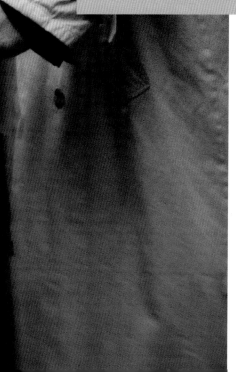

Cars

Cars are one of those personal objects from which others draw impressions. Silly, but true. Men often use this as an excuse to spend far more money on wheels than is sensible.

Not only is this unnecessary; it can also be unwise. Too much car can reflect misplaced priorities, vanity, pretense, stupid debt, or all of the above.

We submit that what you drive is less important than how you maintain it. It's not likely the senior partner will peer beneath the hood to see if you're checking the oil, but he is liable to ride with you to an appointment. If you have to clear a week's worth of newspapers and three empty Starbucks cups from the seat for him to get in, he's not going to be impressed.

Keep your car clean at all times. You never know when you'll have to pick up a client at the airport unexpectedly. Your car is one of those glimpses into the real you that needs to be favorable.

There is also the matter of getting into cars and who sits where. Even if some would argue the political correctness of opening doors for women, we maintain it is viable courtesy.

In a passenger car, whether you are riding or driving, position the most senior person (highest in rank, importance, or age at the moment) in the front seat.

The best practice is to be the last person to get into a cab or car, thus making sure everyone else is comfortable and situated before you are.

HELP WANTED

One true mark of a gentleman is how he treats others—not those "others" who are in positions to better his station in life, but those who aren't. Maître d's, waiters, cab drivers, doormen, janitors, flight attendants, secretaries, clerks, couriers, anyone with whom you come in contact who services you or doesn't have the means or education or opportunities you've had: It's how you talk to and treat these people that shows true character.

An inflated sense of self-importance has defeated many an executive, especially the junior ones. Nothing turns off those above and below you more quickly.

The good news is, one simple rule avoids this pitfall: Never act as if any task or person is beneath you. Get coffee for others and clean up around the coffee station when you do. Help clear the jammed copy machine or answer a ringing phone for someone.

Most of all, treat support personnel as well as you treat executives. This directive is especially important regarding receptionists, secretaries, and administrative assistants. Valued assistants are not only the point of access to the executive office; they also have that executive's ear and often use it to pass on information about the troops. Assistants tend to talk among themselves, too, disseminating information throughout the firm or company. Besides, he or she may be your boss tomorrow. Put bluntly, mistreating anyone is not the way to succeed.

Those who are in positions to better your station in life watch this sort of thing. They notice. If you act surly toward a waiter or cop an attitude toward a secretary, watch out.

Ralph Waldo Emerson once said, "What you do speaks so loud I cannot hear what you say." Social graces, eloquence, and a fine suit can disguise a lack of integrity for only so long. It will eventually be discovered.

CONFIDENCE

We understand the world of business now depends on our ability to connect constantly, quickly, and effectively. That this is possible is a marvelous thing.

At the same time, the devices that allow us these connections have elevated rudeness to unforeseen levels. Or, we should say, the use of these devices.

Since the instruction booklet for cell phones, beepers, Palm Pilots, laptops, and other portable communication devices obviously does not come with those for courtesy and common sense, we are obliged.

The rules are simple:

- Turn the *@$% thing off when you are in the company of another living, breathing person who expects you to be fully engaged with him or her. This includes clients, CEOs, waiters, girlfriends, store clerks, whomever. Turn them off at meetings, restaurants, and any public gathering—especially if there is a performance involved.
- Should you forget to do this and it rings (beeps, buzzes, plays Beethoven's Fifth), don't answer it. By answering it, you are telling present company someone or something is more important.
- Do not talk on the cell phone in public. Everyone can hear you. No one wants to.
- If you must take an urgent call, excuse yourself from the company of others and take your call outside or some place private.

Electronic Comm

Messages

Voice mail and e-mail, vital as they are to today's communication, require their own courtesies and sensibilities. Those weaned on gigabytes of RAM must realize that not everyone in the business world embraces communicating via electronic messaging. Don't assume your contacts do. Be polite. Ask.

Call waiting

Call waiting ranks right up there as a deadly sin of business courtesy. Not only is it offensive to make others wait, but taking the second call tells the first caller something or someone is more important. Nobody likes it. Some will even hang up on you. Good for them.

Never put a caller on hold to take another call. If you must have call waiting, use it only as a signal to check for messages when the current call is finished.

VOICE MAIL

OUTGOING MESSAGE

- Do the world a favor and keep your outgoing message as short as is humanly possible. State your name so the caller knows he or she has the right number. Then ask nicely for the name and number and thank the caller for calling. The reason we have these devices is to save time. The person on the other end of the line is as busy as you are. Speak quickly and to the point and be done with it.

- Avoid the insincere "Your call is important" or "I am currently working with another client" messages. The first sounds patronizing, the second suspicious because you're not always with another client, now, are you? Offer a brief, "I'm sorry I'm unable to take your call," if you must.

- Voice mail messages are impersonal, but that's expected and somewhat accepted today. Make yours the exception by changing it every day to include real information about whether you will be in or out of the office and able to return calls in a timely fashion. People appreciate that.

- We trust you have the good sense to keep business line messages straightforward. But that's also good advice for the home phone. Anything cute or funny is only cute/funny the first time a caller hears it (maybe), and business contacts (like your boss!) will call you at home. Spare them your alter ego/fuzzy family.

- Listen to your voice mail message by calling it. Is this the voice of someone you would want to know? Try speaking with more enthusiasm. This may feel foolish—like you're overdoing it—but some exaggeration is necessary to come across well. Stand up, take a deep breath, and smile as you record. These things infuse the voice with energy.

LEAVING A MESSAGE

- Again, keep it short and simple. Always. If you have a lot to say, save it for the callback. If you don't, people will hear your name and then reflexively hit the "skip" button.

- Begin and end each message by clearly stating your first and last names and your company, if the person you're calling might be unfamiliar. Don't leave him guessing. Never leave just your first name. It's unprofessional.

- Don't assume people have your number. They may be picking up messages from a remote phone. Begin and end the message by clearly and slowly stating the number so the entire message won't have to be replayed to get it. It's also a good idea to state your number twice so people can write accurately. Repetition is always appreciated.

- Never leave a message on voice mail you wouldn't want the world to hear. You can't be sure who is listening.

More and more executives complain about the volume of e-mail they receive. Many confess to not reading much of it. Adding to that volume can irritate clients, customers, and co-workers.

Still, it can be efficient if you use it properly.

- If you want your message to get across, don't rely solely on e-mail. Follow up with a voice mail message stating when you sent the e-mail and briefly what the topic is. Otherwise, it might be deleted.

- Use the subject line. Make sure what you put there won't be misconstrued as junk mail (avoid words like "offer" and "travel"). Put your name in the subject line if it is not part of your return address. Don't write "urgent" unless it truly is.

- As with voice mail, keep the message to a minimum. Make it clear what you want from the recipient (yes or no response? feedback? a meeting time?).

- Although using no uppercasing and other bastardization of spelling and punctuation are somewhat accepted in e-mail, it still looks uneducated and unprofessional. Write an e-mail as you would a letter, minus the heading. Use an open, close, paragraphs, proper punctuation, courtesies, etc. Do not use abbreviations or cryptic symbols and acronyms.

- Nix the smiley faces and other decorations.

- Be aware that e-mail does not carry the inflection and tone of the spoken word. Sometimes what we write comes across as harsh, flip, or critical when that is not our intention. Read and re-read e-mails before sending them to make sure nothing will be misconstrued.

- Never send anything by e-mail you don't want the world to see.

- E-mail does not take the place, nor does it carry the weight, of the handwritten note. However commonly used, e-mail remains somewhat impersonal.

Internal Affairs

Much of what you need to know about how to behave inside the office has already been written here. If you are honest, punctual, courteous, friendly, energetic, thoughtful, helpful, attentive to detail and follow up, a catalyst for introductions but not a conduit for gossip— in short, always maintaining character and looking to make others feel at ease—you will be as successful with co-workers as you are with clients.

That said, following are a few tips worthy of note. Just for good measure.

- Contrary to Hollywood's portrayal, office romance rarely winds up well. More to the point, it can spell disaster emotionally and professionally. Best advice: Shop elsewhere.

- When clients come into your office, treat them like royalty. Greet them as soon as possible in a waiting area or at your office door. Never sit behind your desk as they enter. Always stand and approach with hand extended for a handshake. If possible, sit next to them during the meeting, not across from them behind your desk. Having that big object between you feels intimidating to the client, and face-to-face seating is confrontational.

- Whether leader or participant, do your part to make meetings brief, focused, and productive. Everyone will love you.

- Never assume the head position at a conference table until you have earned it and/or been told to take it.

- Never show the boss disrespect or openly criticize his or her decisions.

- Every office has people who come into your space and won't go away. Avoid this waste of time without being rude by standing up at your desk when they come in—then remain standing. They can't settle in. If they don't get the hint, pick up some papers and start to leave so they have to follow. Never make another person feel dismissed, no matter how badly you want to. And don't waste others' time.

- When traveling with a superior or client, regular rules of rank and conduct still apply. Give the boss the best seats. Open doors. Offer to help with heavy luggage. Mind your manners and your place. Remain professional in conduct and conversation. Just because the two of you are out of town doesn't mean you're suddenly buddies.

- Don't invite a client or co-worker to your hotel room. An innocent invitation can be totally misconstrued.

- It is perfectly acceptable to introduce your spouse, significant other, family, and friends around the office, but be brief and don't make such visits regular events. You're supposed to be working, and others are trying to do the same.

Final Word

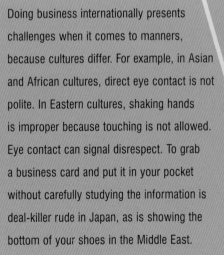

Doing business internationally presents challenges when it comes to manners, because cultures differ. For example, in Asian and African cultures, direct eye contact is not polite. In Eastern cultures, shaking hands is improper because touching is not allowed. Eye contact can signal disrespect. To grab a business card and put it in your pocket without carefully studying the information is deal-killer rude in Japan, as is showing the bottom of your shoes in the Middle East.

Even in the most cosmopolitan cities around the world, certain customs hold strong. It is critical to know them for the same reasons it is critical to know our own: You cannot be effective if your actions show disrespect and make others uncomfortable. Do your homework, and do your best to blend in.

Study and rehearse as you may all the guidelines set forth here, understand there is no way to prepare for every situation. There will be a time when, seated at a crowded round table, you will inadvertently drink from the water glass that belongs to Ms. Big Client seated to your left or make other perhaps more damaging social gaffes.

For these times, one universal rule will see you through. That rule is: Have a sense of humor. When all else fails, humility and a self-effacing attitude remain forever the best rescue.

CONFIDENCE

BLACK TIE

Maybe it's because men equate black tie with parties. It's a logical connection, but not a license to turn sophistication into outlandish. Some legendary fashion mistakes have been perpetrated in the name of semiformal dress: ruffled shirts, jalapeño-covered cummerbunds, salmon dinner jackets. We've seen it all.

The point with black tie is to have a good time, not to look like one. The following offers some healthy boundaries.

The tuxedo/dinner jacket:

• The classic, timeless tuxedo features a single-breasted, one-button black jacket in a year-round, medium-weight worsted wool.

• The lapel can be either shawl or peaked in a dull black satin or silk grosgrain. Buttons match the fabric of the lapel.

• A breast pocket affords the addition of a silk pocket square, but neither is essential.

• Trousers match the jacket with a black satin or grosgrain stripe down the outside of each leg. They can be either pleated or flat front, but they are never cuffed or belted. If they do not remain comfortably around your waist, wear braces.

• Acceptable variations on this classic jacket are the black double-breasted model with peaked lapel or double- or single-breasted with shawl collar.

• A black suit is not a tuxedo and should not be worn as such.

• The white dinner jacket belongs only in truly tropical climates or at summer parties from Memorial Day to Labor Day.

The shirt

- The classic tuxedo shirt is all white with a simple pointed collar like a dress shirt, French cuffs, and studs, not buttons, for closure.
- Most feature narrow vertical tucks or pleats or marcella/pique.
- The wing-tip collar is always popular and is a great second formal shirt to own. The wings can be fussy and unflattering to those with generous necks and/or plump faces. In the event you encounter a winged-collar shirt, however, remember the wings fold in back of the bow tie, not in front.
- The finest shirts (usually custom made) have a button at the bottom that fastens into the trousers to keep everything in alignment. They may also have a camouflaged slit in a side seam so you can reach inside the shirt to thread and secure studs, but this is customized and rare.
- Bibs and ruffles do not belong on tuxedo shirts.
- Color and pattern do not belong on tuxedo shirts. You have outgrown the prom. Haven't you?

DEAL KILLER
OH, SHIRT!

It's 6:00 p.m. Saturday evening before a black-tie dinner and you realize your one and only tuxedo shirt is still at the laundry. Can you get by with a white dress shirt?

Absolutely not.

Dress shirts and formal shirts are not interchangeable. That's why the smart guy plans ahead, owns at least two tuxedo shirts, or befriends someone his size to whom either of these applies.

Bow tie

- A black grosgrain bow tie of moderate proportions is the classic choice.
- Learn to tie a bow tie. It's not that hard and looks much more polished than ready-tied.
- If, after considerable effort, you cannot successfully tie a bow tie, you may wear a ready-tied model. It should never, however, be the clip-on variety. Get one that runs all the way around the neck and hooks discreetly into itself.
- All the obnoxious-pattern rules that apply to regular ties also apply to bow ties. In other words, no seasonal cutesies, no cartoon characters, etc. And nothing that lights up, plays "Jingle Bells," twirls, or squirts water, please.
- As you expand your formal wardrobe, some restrained variations in color and pattern are allowed in bow ties. But be very careful. The tie frames the face, and anything startling upsets the whole look. Not to mention making you look like a big birthday present. If you do venture out from black, the tie should always be a substantial silk or grosgrain in a dark color and pattern intended to flatter the black tux. In other words, no navy-yellow-and-pink paisleys.
- Hollywood and other pools that feed on the fashion-forward have embraced the straight black satin tie with a tuxedo. This is one of those fads best avoided if you want to look your best and not draw unnecessary attention. You risk looking underdressed at best, arrogant at worst.

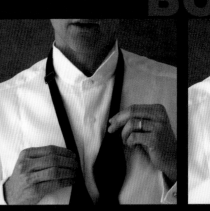

Cummerbund

- First, learn to pronounce the word. It is "cummer," not "cumber," regardless of how you feel in it. Surely you can think of something to help you remember this. It is worn to replace the formal waistcoat and named for a sash worn in India called "kamarband."
- Like the bow tie, the classic cummerbund is black grosgrain. It may also be satin. The same rules of pattern and color apply as stated above for bow ties.
- The pleats in a cummerbund face upward. As legend has it, the design originated to hold opera tickets or catch crumbs.
- The cummerbund should be placed over the lower third of the shirt and cover completely the front of the trouser waist. Too low and the shirt puffs out over. Too high and you risk missing the connection with the trousers.

Pocket square

- A white silk pocket square provides the most sophisticated look.
- A white linen handkerchief is also acceptable, as long as it is pristine.
- Colorful solid or patterned silk pocket squares are best kept to subdued shades and worn with black bow tie and cummerbund.

Formal vest or waistcoat

Another acceptable, if less conventional, look for black tie is to trade cummerbund for a waistcoat, better known as a dress vest.

The classic dress vest mimics the tailcoat with an open front, three low buttons, turned-back lapel, and deep points. A more traditional, high-cut vest—like you would see with a three-piece suit—is also an option.

Like the cummerbund, these vests may offer contrast in a color like deep red, a pattern like brocade, or a fabric like velvet.

The only rule with vests is they must be worn under a single-breasted tuxedo jacket. Most formal waistcoats are made with three buttons and must always be buttoned.

As always, practice restraint and good taste when deviating from solid black.

Studs and cuff links

Studs and cuff links can be purchased in sets. The important note here is that they be small and discreet: No one should ever be able to describe your studs from across the room. Little silver and mother-of-pearl discs are classic, but inexpensive black fabric knots look equally refined.

That said, there is no rule indicating studs and cuff links must match. In fact, some would say mixing makes things more interesting. Keep in mind that studs and cuff links must complement one another, however, and formal cuff links should be no larger than a penny. Studs must all match, and buttons are not acceptable on a tux shirt.

Hosiery

Like other accessories, socks can easily fall prey to that crazy party spirit. Before you know it, little martini glasses will be dancing across your feet.

Before this happens, rush out and buy three pairs of fine-ribbed black socks—not sheer, but thinly woven—that you reserve for black-tie occasions. Congratulate yourself on your exquisite taste.

Shoes

You may have seen a man wearing black velvet pumps emblazoned with family crests or some such and thought them the height of black-tie sophistication. Or maybe you thought he forgot to take off his house slippers.

For both reasons, these velvet ditties—classic as they might be—are best left to Hollywood, the far more seasoned black-tie dandy, or entertaining at home.

Likewise, the opera pump—a patent-leather slip-on with flat grosgrain bow across its low vamp—is another classic that reeks of formal sophistication. But, again, outside of the metropolitan crowd, not many men embrace the look.

The most accepted tuxedo shoe is an elegantly simple, lightweight black patent oxford. If you can't invest in shoes just for evening right now, any plain black oxford or slip-on will do, as long as the sole isn't heavy and there are no perforations (e.g., wing-tips), pronounced flaps, or tassels. A lustrous polish is essential.

PROFESSIONAL ADVICE:

YOUR OWN TUXEDO

There is nothing wrong with renting a tuxedo, provided the formalwear company does an acceptable job of fitting. But it is not an inexpensive proposition. Rent five or six times in your life and you spend close to the cost of purchasing the outfit. It then becomes a wise investment.

Buying also does away with the hassle factor of eternal alterations, making sure all the pieces and parts are there, picking up, returning, etc.

Not to mention wondering where the clothes you're wearing might have slept last weekend.

BRACE YOURSELF

Although braces, or suspenders, are uncommon for business attire, they are perfectly acceptable with a tuxedo. The logic is simple: A belt is not part of the ensemble.

This doesn't mean you can go out and buy a set with Bugs Bunny all over it. *Au contraire.* A straightforward pair of white braces is the sophisticate's choice.

By the way, braces button into one's britches. They never clamp onto them.

We don't care if your last name is McDougal and your ancestors fought at the Battle of Killiecrankie. Unless you were born in Scotland or Ireland, in most parts of the United States kilts as formal attire are not cool. (Well, actually, they can be rather nippy … never mind.) Sean Connery, Mel Gibson, and Liam Neeson may have looked dashing, but the average young man at a metropolitan social occasion in knee socks and a skirt is going to garner more snickers than respect. Save your family plaid until such time that you can wear it in complete confidence and flaunting such an attention-getting getup can work in your favor.

WHITE TIE

Those fortunate enough to receive an invitation to a white-tie event should view it as a gift. Since almost everyone attending will be influential, the evening presents a fine opportunity to build relationships for your future.

If you receive an invitation that specifies "white tie" or "formal attire," the rules are simple and inflexible. You wear what is not-so-affectionately known as a "penguin suit." It consists of:

- black cutaway tailcoat (commonly called "tails") with matching trousers with two narrow satin or grosgrain stripes down the outseams
- white shirt with starched white pique bib, wing collar, and single cuffs fastening with links
- white pique dress waistcoat (commonly called a "vest")
- white pique bow tie
- discreet studs and cuff links
- thin black dress socks
- plain black tuxedo oxfords or pumps

No substitutions allowed.

Why not? Because there are no tasteful variations on white tie. It is meant to be a dress uniform of the highest degree. Every man is supposed to be dressed alike. Those who try otherwise appear foolish.

If it's any consolation, most men look fabulous in white tie.

Where to wear white tie

Fortunately, 99 percent of white-tie or black-tie occasions will say on the invitation which one is required. There's little guesswork.

In the event the invitation says "formal," it usually means white tie. "Semiformal" usually means black tie. When in doubt, however, check. Better to ask than to show up looking foolish.

A sampling of white-tie evenings:

• Some balls, most likely for charity, are white tie, but certainly not all balls. Read the invitation.
• State dinners
• Weddings at or after 7:30 p.m. and only if you are part of the wedding party
• International award ceremonies, like for the Nobel Peace Prize
• Major metropolitan symphony performances, only if you are playing with or conducting same

Only men in this last category or whose social calendar includes many "white-tie" invitations purchase their own white-tie ensemble, usually having it custom made. Most men find it makes more sense to rent.

Renting doesn't mean you settle for inferior fit, however. A few details to note:

• The bottom of the tails should line up with the back of the knees.
• The points of the waistcoat or vest never extend below the points of the tailcoat.
• The points of the tailcoat should lie below the natural waist, not above it.
• The shirt bib does not extend down into the trousers.
• Formal trousers have no cuffs.
• The wings of the shirt fold behind, not in front of, the bow tie.

MAKE THEM DISAPPEAR

Some men who cannot leave well enough alone may be tempted by accoutrements of formal attire, namely the top hat, black walking cane, and/or white scarf.

Restrain yourself, please.

These items do not finish the look as some presume. Instead, they diminish it. They reduce what is the epitome of elegance and good taste to something showy and gauche.

Such things belong only on the cast of *A Christmas Carol* and magicians. Very *good* magicians.

RENT-A-WRECK

We went over this lesson once as it relates to buying suits. It bears repeating here under the heading of "renting formalwear," since it has been the downfall of one too many men: PLAN AHEAD.

You cannot postpone renting a tuxedo or tails until the day of or before the event.

This is not a "same day service" industry. Rental companies need plenty of time to alter and, in some cases, find formalwear that fits as it should for the image you want. Always go in for the first fitting at least a week before the event.

Second rule: Pick up the rental the day before—NOT the day of—the event. If you are renting for an out-of-town event, pick it up one day before your departure date. If any of this results in extra fees, insist on a final fitting a day or two before you need it.

Try on each piece before you leave the shop. Don't trust sizes written on the garments. Mistakes happen. If you have to be at the church in two hours, they may not be able to swap that size 36R jacket for the size 42L you need.

The good news is your friends will be laughing at those photos for years to come.

WHEN THE INVITATION READS

FESTIVE ATTIRE

We would like to say that you should decline any such invitation, because such wording is ambiguous, silly, and overused. But then you would probably miss some great parties.

"Festive" is actually a designation for the women, who find it equally ambiguous and confusing. Men should take their cue from the rest of the invitation, specifically the time and overall tenor of the event. Is it an engraved invitation for a 7:00 p.m. cocktail party at a private club (dark suit and tie) or is it a postcard for a Cinquo de Mayo cookout (sport shirt/linen pants)? For more on interpreting the invitation, see the "What to Wear Where" section, page 210.

BLACK TIE OPTIONAL

Like "festive," "black tie optional" offers more confusion than help on what to wear. It is generally accepted that by placing black tie as an option, the host/hostess/organizers prefer men wear tuxedos.

But men, typically favoring underdressing to overdressing, often forgo the tuxedo for a dark business suit.

If you wear a tuxedo, you are choosing the high road, but you are also risking being only one of a handful dressed this way. Unless you feel certain there will be many men in tuxedos, you may be more comfortable in a dark navy or charcoal suit, white shirt, and dark silk tie. A dark suit is the only appropriate suit, however. A confident man will please the host and wear a tuxedo.

Since dressing for social occasions besides formal ones runs the gamut from dark suits to tan shorts, there is much ground to cover.

The good news is, thanks to Chapter Two, you should already have much of what you need for any semi-formal social occasion (a dark suit) or any dress or sport casual occasion (sports jacket or blazer, shirt, tie, and trousers). Since that chapter so thoroughly covers the dark suit and sports jacket/trouser look, we will not further labor those points here, except to note which ones are appropriate for which occasions.

Instead, we will seek to define what smart casual dressing is and what it is not, at least as applied to the young, ambitious professional.

Understanding casual

In Business Casual, in Chapter Two, we emphasized the importance of maintaining a professional look even though the designation is "casual." That same philosophy applies here. Although your definition of casual may be your cool ripped jeans with a favorite seasoned T-shirt or open collar shirt with the shirttail out, bear in mind these looks may define "dead-beat" for someone who may be key to your future. We don't suggest you give up comfort, but we do recommend you save slovenly for Saturdays at home—and remember that even when you're just running to the store for more beer, you could run into an important client.

Unlike business dressing, there are degrees of casual. The sophisticate differentiates between those degrees and knows when each is appropriate. Casual dress can be broken down into four basic categories, each graduated to a slightly more relaxed look.

Casual

Casual

UNDERSTANDING CASUAL

- As mentioned previously, the elements of **DRESS CASUAL** are the same as those for business casual. The only difference is that business casual may be a suit, whereas dress casual is always a sports coat, trousers, shirt, and tie. For dress casual, the tie may be deleted, a sweater may be added, or a knit polo may be substituted, depending on the occasion. In any case, these looks are dressed and polished.

- **SOCIAL CASUAL** is a step down from dress casual in that the sports coat may be traded for a more functional jacket or sweater and the tie goes. Again, the shirt can be either a regular sport shirt or knit polo. Trousers may graduate from worsted wool to a cotton or twill. The look is still pulled together and crisp, but much more relaxed.

- **WEEKEND CASUAL** is built primarily around denim, cotton, poplin, flannel, and wool. This would be your outdoor looks, summer or winter.

- **ACTIVEWEAR CASUAL** includes the clothes you wear to the gym, the beach, the golf course, the tennis court, or anywhere else where function is as important as style. Although some of these pieces are going to be much dressier than others (trousers and knit polo for golf vs. shorts and a T-shirt for the gym), they all fall under the heading of true sportswear. Of all the categories, this one offers the most opportunities for mistakes, because "functional" can be misinterpreted as "grungy." We assure you that these are not synonyms.

DRESS CASUAL

The good news is what you have already purchased for your business casual wardrobe works for dress social occasions. Your quality year-round navy blazer and worsted gray or tan trousers with a white, blue, or striped dress shirt and tie will take you to most dressy casual social occasions. Your dark suit worn without a tie is also an option here, although it runs second to the sports coat or blazer ensemble in universal acceptability. For more specifics on how to put together this look, see Business Casual in Chapter Two.

One rule of business casual that does not restrict social casual is the use of color. You can get away with a much brighter tie or pocket square for social dressing than you can for business. In fact, color is encouraged in social dressing—not outlandish color, of course, but a touch of brilliance in a tie or pocket square is a good thing. It is what distinguishes this from your more staid biz casual uniform.

As clear-cut as the elements of dress casual are, it often produces the greatest angst for men. Why? Because it's often hard to know when it is appropriate. If you are invited to someone's house for dinner and the hostess says "casual," do you show up in sports coat and tie or something less?

We go into these "what if's" more in depth beginning on page 211, but for now remember the business casual rule: It is better to be overdressed than underdressed. It applies here as well. Whenever you are uncertain, go for coat and tie. You can always remove the tie and/or sports coat to match the level of casual, if warranted. You cannot, however, produce these things out of thin air if everyone else is nattily turned out.

Of course, you can show up in only a shirt and trousers with a coat and tie stashed in the car just in case, but we don't recommend it. Adding clothes on the spot is never graceful.

SOCIAL

SOCIAL CASUAL WARDROBE:

- one pair year-round cotton khaki trousers
- one pair pressed cotton and/or corduroy navy trousers
- three long-sleeved sport shirts in a quiet pattern
- three short-sleeved knit polo shirts in solid colors
- two long-sleeved knit polo shirts or mock turtlenecks in solid colors
- one solid or subtly patterned fine wool pullover sweater
- one solid cotton pullover sweater
- dark navy or forest green socks in a bulkier knit
- brown leather loafers or boat shoes

Social casual

Social casual is a step down from dress casual, but still polished. These are the clothes you might wear to the office on a Saturday, to a sporting event with clients, or on corporate retreats. These aren't your knock-around clothes; that's the next category. These are your comfortable-but-safe clothes.

Every professional's wardrobe should include several pairs of tailored cotton khakis or navy trousers. These will not double as your lie-around-and-watch-football pants. They will remain stain-free and be professionally cleaned and pressed. For lack of a better term, these are your party pants.

Wear these trousers with patterned or solid long-sleeved sport shirts or long- or short-sleeved knit polo shirts. Layer wool or cotton pullover sweaters and add a classic car coat for warmth. Wear a leather belt and loafers, or boat shoes if the occasion is very casual.

When the weather is warm, linen trousers may be introduced into this wardrobe along with lighter cotton shirts. These fabrics can be beautiful, but beware that they wrinkle radically. Just because it is their nature doesn't mean you can get by looking as if you slept in your clothes. Either learn to iron or have these items pressed between wearings. You always want to look crisp and confident.

CASUAL

DEAL KILLER COLLARED

Since you spend working days in a starched collar (we sincerely hope), there is great temptation to pluck weekend sport shirts from the dryer, smooth down the collar with your hands, and head out the door. This is a mistake. The collar is the one thing that should remain pristine in even the most casual looks. A few minutes of pressing make a world of difference in how you look.

DEAL KILLER IRON MAN

Although we stress the importance of avoiding wrinkles throughout casual looks, there is one exception: jeans. Please don't iron them. Crisply creased jeans make the wearer look obsessive-compulsive, anal-retentive, just plain no fun. Pulling warm jeans out of the dryer and folding them gives structure enough to be acceptable.

WEEKEND

These clothes are mostly for those times when you don't expect to encounter clients and superiors, but—as we like to point out—you may. One never knows. That's why it's important to know how to dress well for comfort, too.

Weekend casual is what you wear to do weekend errands, walk the dog, meet friends at a sports bar to watch the game, join your brother at your nephew's soccer match, or help distribute food at a local food bank. It is also what you might wear for summer and winter retreats, après ski, and when a client invites you to his fabulous fishing lodge.

The thing with weekend casual is it's easier to say what it isn't than what it is. It isn't to be confused with slouch, grunge, or any of the other many terms that apply to sloppy dress. It isn't coordinated like social casual, but neither is it thrown together. It's not ironed nor is it rumpled. You look as if you could get dirty, but you don't want to be dirty.

See what we mean?

Basically, weekend casual introduces pieces with pockets: jeans, vests for warmth, chambray shirts and flannel shirts for winter; cargo shorts, fly-fishing shirts, rain-repellent windbreakers for summer. Although these pieces have no place in a traditional work setting, they may be perfectly acceptable in specific social situations, even with colleagues or clients. More on this in the next section.

The good news about this category is it is very masculine, and the combination of rich textures and color is flattering. The main thing to remember here is you never want to look sloppy. Jeans should never be ripped, discolored, or dirty. Shirttails should be tucked in. Knit shirts and cotton shorts shouldn't look too-long-in-the-dryer rumpled (cargo shorts are particularly bad about this). Flannels shouldn't look faded. Shoes should never look worn. You get the picture.

This is perhaps the riskiest category of all because many men make the mistake of thinking it doesn't matter what they wear to play and exercise.

The potential to sweat is not a license to dress like a derelict, however. Torn, stained, or tacky T-shirts and baggy sweatpants left over from college are never acceptable for workouts, unless you are at home with the blinds closed.

But neither do you have to go to the gym in tailored shorts and a polo shirt. Simply make sure exercise clothes look fresh and clean and fit you comfortably. Shoes shouldn't look like marathon blowouts. Ditch the T-shirts with slogans and patterned shorts or pants. Ditto for sleeveless or strappy T-shirts, regardless of how great your biceps are. We don't care. Look respectable, even as you sweat.

Sweats, shorts, T-shirts, bathing suits, and athletic shoes should hold to the same standard as the rest of your professional wardrobe: Specifically, you wouldn't be embarrassed if your boss/top client/future father-in-law saw you dressed like this.

As for specific sports, there are often dress codes. You will find more on this in the following section of what to wear where.

ACTIVEWEAR
Golf, Running, Sports

DEAL ■KILLER
TACKY T'S

Just as the wise man is careful about what he says, he should be equally careful about what his T-shirts say. What you think is clever someone else might find offensive. A discreet school logo (providing you actually attended this school) is okay, but save the beer logos and Cancun souvenir shirts for couch potato days.

Play it safe and stock up on solid T-shirts in navy and other becoming colors for workouts and other such endeavors. Stay away from solid white, however, which is strictly reserved for underwear, as in "under" what you "wear."

DEAL ■KILLER
UNSUITABLE

The only suitable bathing suit is a modest one. Even if you hold the current American record in backstroke, it's no excuse to show up at a social function near water wearing a Speedo or lycra in any shape or form. Every man's activewear wardrobe needs one boxer- or surfer-type bathing suit in a solid color.

A WORD "ACCESSORIES"

We have already touched on some accessories in our explanations of the various degrees of casual, but let's spend a little time getting specific here. The good news is there is very little to consider.

Shoes

Here we go again with shoes, but it can't be overstated: Shoes are important.

Just as you can't wear running shoes with your charcoal suit, you can't wear black wingtips to the company picnic. Well, you can, but you'll look pretty silly. That's why it is important to have an acceptable leather casual shoe in the wardrobe. The rubber-soled brown loafer commonly known as a boat shoe is safe and seasonless.

Also beware the definition of "casual shoe." It could be interpreted as anything from black canvas high-top sneakers to outlandish two-tone European lace-ups with squared-off toes to flip-flops. Don't get sucked into the selection. If your wardrobe follows the conservative guidelines set forth here, your shoes should, too. Back to the boat shoe or a reasonable facsimile thereof for a go-anywhere staple. Flip-flops may feel great, but they're only for the beach or the gym shower.

If your black dress shoe is an oxford, consider investing in a black leather loafer to wear with your wool trousers for dress and social casual. If your casual wardrobe leans more toward browns and beige, choose a brown loafer instead. An oxford in brown leather or suede is also good to own for casual dress, but not essential.

Every man needs a decent pair of classic sneakers, preferably in leather, for weekend and activewear only. But be cautious about pairing them with tailored trousers or dark jeans. Light shoes—especially chunky ones—beneath dark trousers is a decidedly unsophisticated look.

That's why we recommend a good lace-up leather walking shoe for the casual wardrobe. It does the job of a sneaker, but looks good with khakis and jeans. Boat shoes can serve this purpose, but they may not provide enough foot support for a day of sightseeing.

As for sandals, we must confess we have never met one we liked. The Romans may have worn them well, but they look about as cool on today's man as the toga. The only possible exception is the classic fisherman's sandal. Even so, we recommend it be worn primarily in the tropics with linen trousers and a fabulous silk shirt. Some guys can get away with it. Others can't.

Sandals are fashion-forward and are worn without socks with shorts or very light summer casual slacks.

Socks

Delicately knit dress hosiery does not belong with casual shoes. Even the leather boat shoe calls for a heavier knit sock, although it can be dark.

There are a few other sock absolutes to remember. Repeat after us, please:

"I will never, ever wear a dark sock with a light shoe, especially sneakers."

"I will never, ever wear a dark sock with shorts."

"I will never, ever wear socks with sandals (if I dare wear sandals)."

"I will never, ever wear white socks with dark dress shoes." (OK, so Letterman does it. When you are a legendary late-night talk show host, you can do it, too.)

"I will never, ever go sockless to a dressy social occasion."

Hats

As opposed to a ball or golf cap, if you are dressed in a sports coat, you need to stick with a business hat. That means a brimmed fedora. Driving caps are also classic, but less conventional unless you are European or elderly.

For all other levels of casual, plain knit stocking caps are OK for extreme cold. Avoid perky patterns. Hats with earflaps, however tempting, are not advisable as they tend to diminish IQ. Ditto for earmuffs. That said, if you are going to a Packers game in late December, you may be forgiven the flaps. But carry a good sense of humor.

Ball caps have become a popular and acceptable accessory for weekend and active looks. They can be essential for convertibles, watching sports outdoors, and any other occasion where the sun is liable to either burn you or make you squint like Forrest Gump.

Gloves

A pair of leather dress gloves in brown or black complements all levels of casual. But if you need something a bit more functional, a pair of synthetic fleece or insulated ski gloves in a dark color is acceptable. Under no circumstances beyond shoveling snow do you wear mittens.

BALL CAP DO'S AND DON'TS

- Do not wear a ball cap (or any other hat) indoors. Hats indoors not only look inappropriate, but they are still viewed as disrespectful by some.

- Do be aware that ball caps obscure your eyes and inhibit eye contact. If you are meeting someone, it is good form to remove the cap while you shake hands.

- Don't turn the ball cap around backwards unless you wish to look juvenile and stupid.

- Do keep your cap in pristine shape—no frayed edges or smudgy brims.

- Do pay attention to fit. The cap must fit down over the crown of your head snugly, and the brim must be curled downward to frame your face. Store the brim in a coffee mug to keep the perfect curl. Go for too-tall crowns and flat brims only if you're entertaining truck drivers.

- Do choose tasteful hats. As with T-shirts, beware the ball cap's message—nothing cutesy or offensive. Any logo should be embroidered, not stamped on the crown.

CARRY ALL

Often a man's workout requires that he carry athletic clothes to and from the office. Don't take this lightly. The bag you carry factors into your professional image. Toting your togs in a bright nylon tote covered in logos does nothing for that. Besides, you should be low-key about your extracurriculars, even if they are healthy.

Invest in a plain black or dark brown overnight bag, sports bag, or messenger bag just large enough to accommodate your stuff, but no larger. You want it to catch as little attention as possible when you carry it.

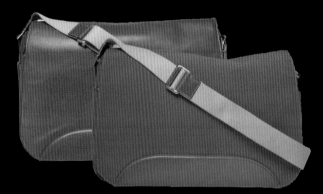

We have come up with a wide variety of likely social situations in which a professional might find himself—as well as a few unlikely ones—and guidelines for dressing accordingly. If your particular invitation does not appear here, we are hopeful something close enough to it does so you might be well informed and well uniformed.

That said, we also understand how disinclined male Homo sapiens is toward soliciting directions, be they geographical or personal. All we can say to that is, "Get over it." The gentleman who asks and shows up dressed appropriately appears far more savvy than the one who refuses to make that phone call and suffers the consequences of his pride.

What to Wear

When the boss is present…

No one phrase changes the rule of dress so abruptly as this one. If it is likely you will encounter your superior(s) or important clients at any given social event, you must dress more conservatively and carefully. Now it is not just play; it is work. We don't suggest you don your navy suit for a trip to the stadium. That would look foolish. But wearing jeans and a sweatshirt appears equally foolish.

Whenever you expect your professional self to come under scrutiny, go to your dress casual wardrobe. You won't regret it. Leave the tie behind if—and only if—you are certain it would look out of place.

When you are the host…

The good host wants his guests to feel comfortable. The best way to do that is to state clearly the evening's attire during the invitation process. (For example, "It's comfortable casual, so leave your ties at home." "It's a hayride. Wear jeans." "It's black tie.") But when the event is somewhat nebulous, the host must be careful to set an inclusive tone. Try to strike a middle ground with your clothing so you will be neither more nor less dressed up than your guests. For most such casual occasions, wool, cotton, or linen trousers (depending on season), sport or dress shirt without a tie, and maybe a sweater makes host and guests alike feel appropriately dressed. Unless it is a dressed-up coat-and-tie occasion, the host should not wear a sports coat. It looks presumptuous in one's own home.

To dinner at someone's home…

If that home belongs to a superior or client, this is business, not social. You must not only comport yourself as you would around these people in a business setting; you must also dress with the same care.

If business is the reason for the social occasion, wear your dark suit. If you are told it is "casual," wear a sports coat or blazer, dress shirt, wool trousers, and tie.

The only exception is if you are specifically told, "It's a barbecue. Dress casually." In that case, choose social casual, but nothing sportier than that.

If that home belongs to someone you know only casually, dressing well shows respect. Again, blazer, trousers, solid shirt, and tie is safe. If you are certain this is overdressed, leave off the tie but maintain the rest of the outfit. At any level of casual, a blazer or sports coat is a good touch. It adds class with jeans if the evening is decidedly dressed down.

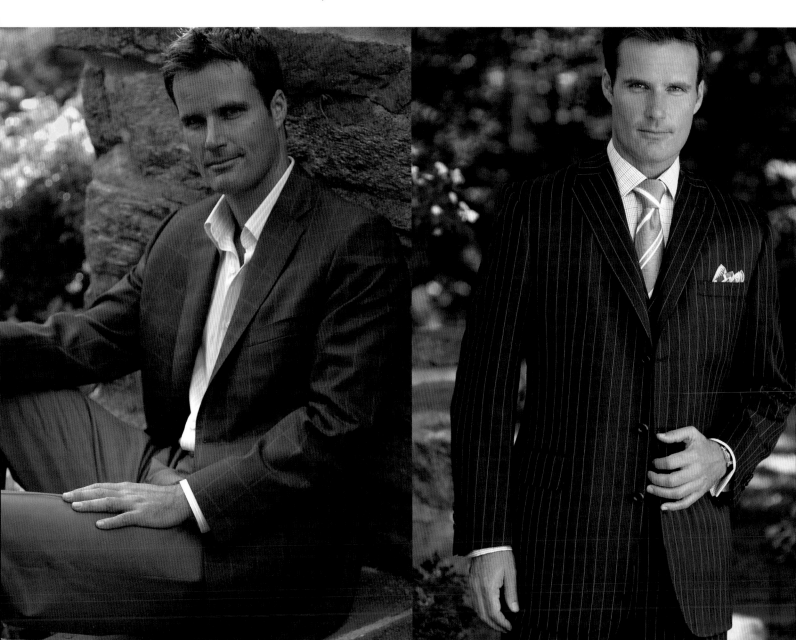

If the dinner celebrates a special occasion, like a holiday, graduation, engagement, or even an important birthday, wear a tie. Special occasions warrant special attire, unless you are specifically instructed otherwise. Remember, you can always remove the tie.

To meet her parents…
Treat this as you would dinner with the boss. In both cases, your future is at stake. Ask her for detailed instructions (that is not just "coat and tie" but "your Tom James button-down collared white shirt fresh from the laundry with the navy and red striped tie, …) and do not improvise.

When the invitation says "business attire"…
Wear a dark suit with a white or light blue shirt and conservative tie. Treat it like an important client meeting.

When the invitation says "business casual"...
This means a sports coat or blazer, but a tie is not necessary. Still, you may wear one.

When the invitation says "semiformal"...
This translates to "suit with tie."

When the invitation says "festive attire"...
Don't get excited. This designation is primarily for women, who are as clueless as you are, if that helps. It is sometimes appended to seasonal black-tie events, which means you can wear your holiday bow tie and cummerbund if you must. Or it may be used for luaus, granting permission to drag out the Hawaiian print shirt. Our advice is to resist on both occasions and stick with what you know to be in good taste.

When the invitation says "cocktail attire"...
This does not mean black tie. If an event is black tie, it will clearly state that on the invitation. Therefore, "cocktail" indicates dark suit and tie. In larger metropolitan areas like Los Angeles or New York, the more fashion-forward might go dark-suit-no-tie for cocktail. We don't recommend it, since it can come off as trendy and underdressed.

For holiday dinners...
Just as "dinner with the boss" pumps up formality a notch or two, so does the word "holiday." People tend to dress up more during the holidays, and you should, too. This is a special time of year with special occasions. Holiday parties and dinners call for a sports coat and tie, at least. A suit is also acceptable. If the invitation specifies "casual," even that should be ratcheted up a notch. Stick with dress casual.

To church...
The term "Sunday best" has all but lost its meaning in many parts of the country and in many churches these days. Blue jeans have become as common as suits in many houses of worship. However, don't assume that's the case should you be invited to church or decide to visit one on your own. Some congregations still adhere strictly to the coat-and-tie model as respectful dress. That's what you should wear until you are certain something less is acceptable. Note: While hats should always be removed indoors, this is especially critical inside a church. It demonstrates respect. The only exception is the yarmulke at Jewish services.

To a bar mitzvah or bat mitzvah...
The suit and tie are most appropriate, although a blazer, trousers, and tie will pass. Today, most congregations do not require a yarmulke, or skullcap, to be worn inside the synagogue. But congregations that do hold to this tradition provide one to visitors as they enter. You must take it and wear it, even if you are not Jewish. It is a sign of respect.

To a televised awards show...

If your girlfriend is up for best actress (no comment), you should wear black tie. The same applies if you are (a) a certifiable part of the industry being honored, (b) seated where the television cameras will likely be on you, or (c) headed for ritzy after-parties where most of the guests will be dressed formally. If the invitation specifies black tie, it's a no-brainer.

But if you are going to the Grammy Awards because you have several clients in the music industry and you will be seated well outside the VIP section, a dark suit and tie is appropriate. In this case, to wear black tie would be masquerading as something you are not. When in doubt, ask.

To an awards banquet...

If the invitation specifies "black tie," that is what you wear. If it does not, you will be fine in a dark suit and tie. If you are speaking at this event or seated at a head table, it bears inquiry as to whether or not black tie is appropriate, even though the invitation does not state this.

To a charity fund-raising dinner...

This calls for suit and tie, unless the invitation specifies black or white tie.

To a wedding…

What you wear to a wedding depends mostly on the time of day it takes place and, in some cases, the spirit of the nuptials. For example, there are those who get married on the beach at sunset and want everyone to be casual and barefoot. (Even so, you will be more appropriate—and apt to wind up with the good-looking bridesmaid—if you wear beige linen pants and a white linen shirt instead of cargo shorts and a polo.) Then again, some beach weddings are the height of formality. This is one of those instances when it is essential to ask. In fact, it is always permissible to ask the bride or groom. You do not appear stupid; you appear thoughtful.

Generally speaking, any wedding before 7:00 p.m. calls for a suit and tie. Black tie is only appropriate for weddings at or after 7:00 p.m. If the invitation is formal and engraved (*Dr. and Mrs. Martin Edward Heffington III request the honor of your presence…*"), the reception is held at a private club or hotel ballroom, and the bride and groom come from families accustomed to formal dress, expect a black-tie crowd. Unfortunately, the invitation never specifies.

The good news is these days you will likely find many men in dark suits even at formal weddings. This is acceptable, especially if the suit is navy and you accent with a crisp white shirt and conservative tie. It's the next best thing to black tie.

White tie is never appropriate for a wedding unless you are part of the wedding party and it is requested by the bride or bride's mother.

To a funeral...

The object here is not to draw attention to oneself, but to be there for others. Hence, this is not the place for your bright necktie and perky pocket square. Your darkest suit, white shirt, and a quiet tie compose the most appropriate ensemble.

To the White House...

Dress Presidentially: Dark suit, starched white shirt, and conservative tie for any occasion except a formal State Dinner. That calls for black tie. They'll let you know. Trust us.

Dining at a private club or country club...

Many clubs have dress codes that often vary depending on time of day and in which part of the club you will dine. Country club dining options may range from an informal grill where golfers eat before and after playing, to a slightly more formal family dining room, to an even more upscale adults-only bar and dining area, to a formal coat-and-tie-required dining room. It is easy enough to call the club in question and inquire about dress requirements.

In any case, it is good form to wear a coat and tie to dine at any private club, even if you sense the gathering is informal. You don't want to risk being turned away due to inappropriate dress, and no guest should challenge the rules, regardless of how archaic he believes them to be.

Obviously, if you are going there to play golf or tennis, dress for the game. But if you will be eating before or after, make sure you have a sports jacket, fresh shirt, and trousers in case your host or hostess has reserved a spot in one of the dining rooms.

To an art opening ...

It depends on the time, the gallery, and how formal the event. If it is an exclusive gallery or museum and this is strictly an invitation-only evening event, a dark suit and tie are appropriate. If it is a smaller gallery, the art is contemporary and the crowd will be young, sports coat/no tie is safe.

To the theater, opera, ballet, or classical concert...

Like today's church, our theaters, opera houses, and symphony halls have seen a marked decline in the formality of how patrons dress. One used to wear black tie to these venues, but now that would seem dramatically overdressed. Although many show up in sweaters, knit polos, and casual trousers, you will exude much more class in a blazer or sports coat over an open collared shirt. The tie is not necessary, but it is a fine touch.

   If it is a special performance and/or a renowned venue, like an opening night on Broadway or at the Metropolitan Opera or the Bolshoi Ballet performing at Lincoln Center, a tie is in order.

To the company picnic...

Don't let "picnic" lull you into cutoffs and flip-flops. This is no time to be sprawling on a blanket. Any company function is business, even picnics. Wear a polo shirt and cotton khaki slacks with leather belt and shoes if all you plan to do is eat and socialize. Trade the slacks for tailored shorts and the loafers for presentable sneakers if there are games like softball. You do want to be a good sport. If you wear sneakers, remember white cotton socks. No sandals, please.

To a reception...

There are receptions for many different reasons, some business, some social. The degree of formality varies. A reception for a new business, for example, scheduled for 5:00 p.m. on a Thursday expects attendees to come from work. Therefore, a suit and tie or sports coat and tie are appropriate.

But a reception for a visiting dignitary calls for a higher degree of formality. Only a dark suit and tie are acceptable.

Then there is the informal Friday evening reception for a colleague joining the firm. That might be a sports coat/trouser/no tie affair.

In general, if the reception is immediately following working hours on a weekday, wear business attire unless "casual" is specified. If it is a decidedly casual social affair, you may ditch the tie. But if the invitation is engraved and the event sounds important, the dress code will likely be more formal.

To a brunch...

The formality or informality of a brunch is typically dictated by the event it precedes or celebrates. A wedding brunch usually means suit or sports coat and tie, as does a brunch after church for a christening. But a brunch at someone's home before a football game is more casual: sports coat and wool trousers, no tie. Good clue: If you receive a formal printed invitation and the brunch takes place at a private club or some other upscale venue, wear a tie.

When you travel...

Comfort has become the order of the day on airplanes, and who can blame us? But if you want to be treated well when you travel, dress well. It doesn't take much to distinguish oneself amid all the denim and fleece. You may even get bumped up to first class.

Yachting…

Spare us the double-breasted navy blazer with gold buttons and white trousers. Just because some wealthy someone invited you aboard the yacht doesn't make you Thurston Howell III. If you are sailing and are likely to take an active part, a polo shirt, tailored shorts (for a warm day), and either boat shoes or another canvas or light leather shoe with a white rubber sole is the perfect ensemble. Never wear athletic shoes with dark or colored soles on a boat as they may leave dark scuffs on the deck. Take along sunglasses, sunscreen, a baseball cap, and a cotton sweater or windbreaker in case it gets breezy. But if the only thing you'll be hoisting is a cocktail, trade the shorts for trousers in cooler climates.

To a barbecue…

Any mention of the great outdoors on an invitation usually lowers the degree of casual a notch, the exception being a garden party, which can be a suit-and-tie affair. You never wear a tie to a barbecue, but whether it calls for shorts or something dressier can be a toss-up. The safest ensemble is pressed khakis and a professionally laundered sport shirt or knit polo. If there will be clients and colleagues—especially elders—in the mix, bring along a sports coat just in case.

To a pool party…

This is tricky, because there are pool parties where everyone stands around the flickering tiki torches sipping mojitos in their linen best. Then there are pool parties where everyone is in the pool. Major difference in attire.

It is always best to assume it is the former type of pool party, but have your bathing suit (conservative trunk style in a solid color, please) and flip-flops in the car in case it is the latter.

To a beach party…

See "pool party."

To a resort…

Just because it is vacation doesn't mean you take leave of your sense of class. Knit polo shirts and lightweight wool, cotton, or linen trousers are a must for resort wear. Shorts should be tailored and knee-length. T-shirts should be reserved for your morning run on the beach. Always take a sports coat or blazer that works with your trousers since some resorts require guests to dress for dinner.

On a cruise…

Information outlining appropriate dress for a particular cruise should be provided by the cruise line. Most cruises these days are largely resort casual. That means knit polos and linen or fine cotton sport shirts; tailored shorts; trousers in cotton, lightweight wool, or linen; a blazer and/or sports coat for most dinners; and a sweater or two for breezy days on deck.

But take note: There will be one or maybe two formal nights where guests are expected to dress in black tie. Honor this, if possible. Since many guests settle for a suit or less for these dinners, it is easy to distinguish yourself by dressing beautifully. If you happen to be asked to sit at the captain's table, you will be glad you have your formalwear. Ships with a tropical course love their guests in white dinner jackets on the upper-class decks.

For a weekend in the Hamptons …
It doesn't have to be the Hamptons. It could be an invitation to someone's mountain house, lake cabin, or condo at the beach. The main thing to focus on in all cases is being prepared for whatever might come up. This isn't as hard as it may sound.

If you are going somewhere where you are likely to go to restaurants, clubs, a party, or some other event, make sure you have a sports jacket and tie. Otherwise, pack one change of trousers and shorts, three polo shirts, one freshly laundered sport shirt, underwear, and whatever activewear you might need to cover beach/golf/tennis/sailing/hiking activities.

Don't burden your hosts with luggage, but take enough so you can have a few changes. No one wants to do laundry, nor do they want to see you in the same shirt for three days.

Unless you are going to a cabin in the woods or some other remote location where weekend casual rules, take a sports coat or blazer. You never know when you'll need it.

To see a pro team play…
This varies somewhat by sport and the caliber of seats you will occupy. If you are going to sit in the owner's box at an NFL game, sports jacket and tie. In fact, any VIP box requires a sports jacket and tie.

But not all boxes are VIP. Many corporations and individuals own boxes at arenas and stadiums for entertaining. Each sets the tone for that particular box. In general, people dress up more for box sitting, but not a lot more. Our advice is social casual: sports coat with sport shirt or polo and khakis or corduroy trousers. Leave the tie at home.

If you are sitting in regular seats, the sports coat is not necessary even if you are keeping company with executives or clients. You don't want to look like you're trying too hard. But even in weekend casual clothes (sweater, wool jacket, flannel shirt, etc.), khakis or corduroys look better than traditional jeans.

If the weather is -3 degrees, dress appropriately. Staying warm doesn't necessarily mean looking ridiculous if you layer, beginning with good thermal underwear and ending with warm gloves, wool scarf, and knit hat. But no one will fault you for breaking style rules under extreme conditions.

By the way, face paint is never the right accessory.

To play golf or tennis at a private club…

Some clubs require tennis players to dress in white only and wear collared shirts (i.e., no T-shirts) on the courts. Most clubs also require collared shirts on the golf course and a few even prohibit shorts. Today even the most exclusive clubs may allow shorts, but never anything denim. Ask a member or call the pro shop.

To play golf, tennis, squash, handball, etc., at a public facility…

Even if you are not playing at a private club, appropriate dress is still important, especially if you may encounter clients or superiors. Wear the clothing of the sport in which you are participating, not whatever happens to be clean in your casual drawer. No cargo shorts and T-shirt on a tennis court or jeans and oxford cloth dress shirt on the golf course. Wear a collared shirt (primarily white) and tailored shorts for the court and a long- or short-sleeved polo shirt and pressed slacks for the golf course. If you look like a pro, maybe you will play like one.

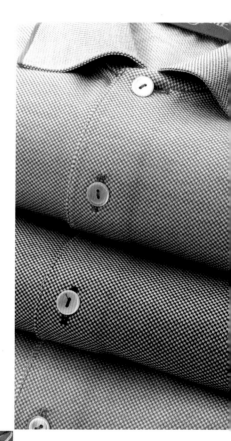

Skiing...

The good news about ski resorts is that even the most upscale welcome very casual dress at lodges and restaurants. Jeans, snow-worthy boots, rich flannel shirts, heavy jackets, beefy sweaters, and down vests are common and acceptable wherever. This is home for weekend casual. Guests at ski resorts don't distinguish themselves by dressing up, but rather by how they dress down. Expect fur, beautiful leathers, and cashmere with denim at the more exclusive resorts—on both men and women.

Hunting...

If you are invited to the boss's cabin for a (fill-in-the-blank) hunt, go to a store that sells attire for that particular type of hunting. They will help you.

But realize this doesn't mean you will spend the entire weekend clad in camouflage. Please. When you are not hunting, elements of a weekend casual wardrobe work just fine, with the possible exception of jeans. A pair of corduroy trousers may look more polished at a lodge dinner after a day of hunting or fishing.

Fly-fishing...

Again, consult a fly-fishing store or check one out on line. Think tan, khaki, and sun protection. The good news is you can rent many of the essentials like waders and a vest from a guide or fly-fishing store. What you wear beneath these garments depends on the season. Quick-drying fabrics (not cotton) are preferable, since winding up in the water is always a distinct possibility.

To the horse races...

If it is one of the Triple Crown events or a prestigious steeplechase race, the gentry will wear sports coats and ties. This is the perfect place for a livelier dress shirt or your most colorful tie and pocket square, since bright silks are integral to the festivities. If you are going as part of the masses tailgating in the infield or on the periphery, a polo or sport shirt and trousers suffice. But, again, a sports coat always looks good.

At a dude ranch...

Don't laugh. Ranch vacations are very popular these days, and some of them are quite upscale. Although jeans and cowboy boots are always a part of the experience, some ranches expect guests to dress up a bit for dinner—as in nicer jeans and better shirts. Read the ranch brochure carefully before you pack. It should give guidelines. Call ahead; it works well.

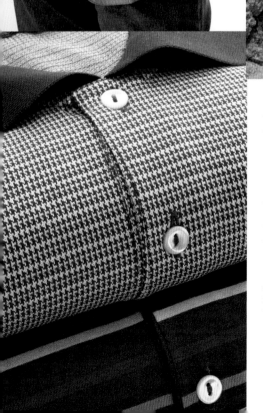

A Final Word

on casual dressing and social graces...

Despite your best efforts (and ours) to ensure you are always appropriately attired whatever the occasion, there may be times when you miss the mark. Never fear. The manner in which you handle these missteps can do more to enhance your image than any fine cashmere blazer.

If you find yourself either underdressed or overdressed, do not draw attention to that fact by profuse apology. If you are wearing jeans and everyone else is wearing ties, one brief word of apology to the host or hostess will suffice. Then say nothing else about it. Do not appear self-conscious. Simply behave as confidently as if you are appropriately dressed.

If some boor insists on drawing attention to your gaffe, be ready with self-effacing humor. In the case of overdress, something like, "You didn't know? I'm your maître d' this evening!" In the case of underdress, "I'm sorry about this. I thought it was a garden party—the kind where we plant things."

We've all heard the stories. Some bright young associate with a promising career makes a fool of himself at a high-profile holiday party. Instead of a Christmas bonus, he receives a pink slip.

Social suicide happens. Let's avoid its happening to you.

Life is not all business—thank goodness—but how you conduct yourself in nonbusiness settings is also important to your career. On the path to success, knowing how to be a celebrated host and a welcomed guest can prove invaluable.

Such acclaim isn't simply a matter of not doing the wrong thing; it is also doing the right thing.

We're here to help.

In fact, we already have. Much of what you need to know about social confidence you learned in Chapter Three: the proper way to greet and introduce people; how to engage in conversation and share a meal; courtesies like writing follow-up notes, opening doors, and turning off cell phones. The information in this chapter merely adds to your repertoire of how to put others at ease and do the same for yourself.

As we pointed out, much of this acumen comes naturally if a man remains thoughtful. Using the wrong size wine glass is easily forgiven, but lapses in character and kindness are not. So long as you endeavor to treat others as you would be treated, you already have the most important part down.

Invitations

Responding

If you gain one thing from this section, let it be this: Always respond promptly to invitations.

The letters "RSVP" on an invitation stand for *répondez s'il vous plaît*. Translated from French, it means "please respond."

Far too many people ignore this request, which is the worst sort of rudeness toward the host. People who would never ignore a verbal invitation will ignore written ones. There is no difference between the two.

Still others think *RSVP* means respond only if you're coming. They are misinformed. *RSVP* means "let the host know if you are or are not attending." Period. Any questions?

Furthermore, don't wait until the Friday before a Saturday event to respond. Respond as quickly as possible, certainly within forty-eight hours of receiving the invitation. If there are extenuating circumstances that keep you from knowing whether or not you can attend, communicate this. People planning parties or other activities are going to a lot of trouble and probably expense. A late response insults their efforts.

Even if the "host" is a group, organization, or business, the rules for responding still apply. It may be a huge event, but someone is in charge of planning. He or she deserves the courtesy of knowing how many to expect.

In the case of the big party or reception you might think, *"They won't miss me if I don't show."* Think again. Your unclaimed name tag may be sitting lonely on a table throughout the event where all can witness your bad manners.

HOW TO RESPOND

A

"<Your first and last name> is pleased to accept Mr. Perky's kind invitation for Saturday, July 12, at Ritzy Manor."

B

"<Your first and last name> regrets that he is unable to accept Mr. Perky's kind invitation for Saturday, July 12."

C

Dear Dan,

Thanks for the invitation to dinner Saturday, June 8, at 7:00 p.m. I am looking forward to being there.

Butch

- Below the RSVP on a printed invitation, there may be a phone number or e-mail address, in which case a phone call or e-mail is the preferred means of response.

- If there is no number or enclosure card for response, assume the host expects a written response. This is rare these days, but not extinct. If it is a formal occasion, respond as in either A or B (above). That's all. Write this by hand on a blank piece of stationery or a plain formal card, and mail it. If the occasion is informal but a written response is expected, you may reply as in C (above).

- If in place of *RSVP* the invitation reads *"Regrets Only,"* then respond only if you will not attend.

- If there is no *RSVP* or *Regrets Only*, there is no obligation to respond. Be a nice guy and respond anyway. The host will appreciate it.

- If you have been invited to a party you must pay to attend, like a charity event, your check serves as your response. Send it in as quickly as possible in consideration of the organizers, but no need to send formal regrets unless so requested on the invitation.

BOTTOM LINE

Those who do not respond to invitations in a timely manner will cease to receive them. If that is your intent, there are more genteel ways to go about it than being labeled inconsiderate and rude.

WELL STOCKED

The quality of the paper you use to pen a note or letter can say as much about you as the words upon it.

Locate a store that specializes in fine paper. Ask the salesperson to show you all-purpose blank cards and stationery in a quality heavy stock.

Stick with off-white (called "ecru") or a quiet shade of gray. Both are masculine. Avoid bright white for personal stationery as it resembles fax paper. White is fine for cards, however.

Buy the best paper you can afford and plenty of it. If you want to personalize your stationery, engraving first and last names or initials provides a nice touch. Either should be relatively small and done in a masculine block script in dark ink. Tone-on-tone, such as raised ecru script on ecru paper, is another classic look.

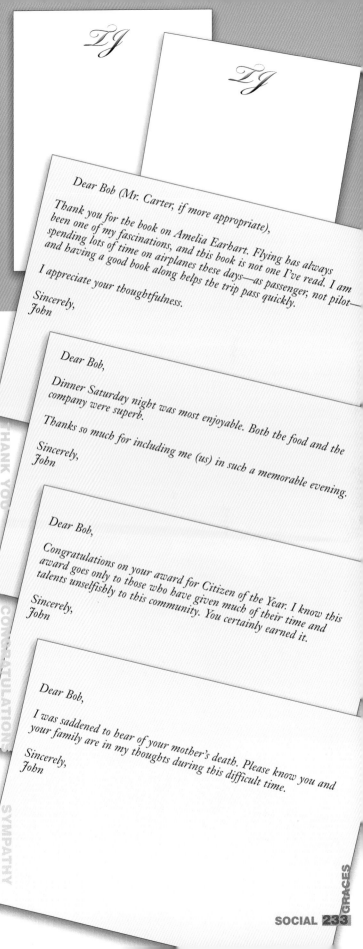

Dear Bob (Mr. Carter, if more appropriate),

Thank you for the book on Amelia Earhart. Flying has always been one of my fascinations, and this book is not one I've read. I am spending lots of time on airplanes these days—as passenger, not pilot—and having a good book along helps the trip pass quickly.

I appreciate your thoughtfulness.

Sincerely,
John

Dear Bob,

Dinner Saturday night was most enjoyable. Both the food and the company were superb.

Thanks so much for including me (us) in such a memorable evening.

Sincerely,
John

Dear Bob,

Congratulations on your award for Citizen of the Year. I know this award goes only to those who have given much of their time and talents unselfishly to this community. You certainly earned it.

Sincerely,
John

Dear Bob,

I was saddened to hear of your mother's death. Please know you and your family are in my thoughts during this difficult time.

Sincerely,
John

Write on

The reason we suggest buying a quantity of good paper is because you'll need it. We hope.

As discussed in Chapter Three, penning notes by hand to express thanks, congratulations, or condolences is a waning art. That's precisely why you should make a habit of it. People no longer expect such a note as obligation, so they view it as a special and meaningful gesture.

Yet many men would rather have gum surgery than compose a note. They're not mean people; they're just unsure of what to say and afraid of sounding inappropriate or silly. Let us put those fears to rest right now: What you write is far less significant than the fact you write at all. People will be touched by your kindness and effort regardless of your words.

Second, the best notes are simple ones. There is no need for flowery language or lengthy essays. Keeping the note cordial and brief is perfectly acceptable.

Here we offer a few examples of brief, appropriate notes. They are intended as inspirations, not blueprints. Make each note authentically your own.

Happy endings

Ending a note with "Sincerely" is always safe, but may sound too impersonal if you know the recipient well.

Other acceptable—but not too intimate—closings are "Best wishes," "Regards," "Best," and "Cordially." Obviously, do not use anything chipper like "Best wishes" on a sympathy note. If you know the bereaved well, you may close with something more personal and sentimental like "Warmest regards."

[For more examples and instruction, we recommend *A Gentleman Pens a Note: A Concise, Contemporary Guide to Personal Correspondence* by John Bridges and Bryan Curtis, Rutledge Hill Press.]

There comes a time in most men's lives when it is appropriate to propose a toast. Since this is a form of public speaking, it scares us more than impotence and a disastrous drop in the stock market combined.

Compounding this fear is the fact toasts are given at emotional times—weddings, anniversaries, birthdays, graduations. No man wants to stand at the microphone and sob, and many fear they will.

While only the most clever and seasoned deliver the perfect toast without butterflies, the rest of us can be competent participants in this tradition by following a few guidelines.

MAKING TOASTS

DEAL **KILLER**
THE TOASTED TOASTER

If toasts are in order, stay sober. You may think the alcohol will fortify you for the spotlight, but it will more likely make you ramble on too long, forget key points (like *names*), jumble the sentiment, and generally embarrass yourself. Exercise restraint. Back away from the Champagne.

- First and foremost, speak from the heart. Even if it isn't the most eloquent toast, it will be the most touching.

- The first toast always sounds good because there's nothing for comparison. Don't be afraid to kick things off.

- Like so much in life, short and simple works best. Unless you are an adept and celebrated public speaker, a long toast makes everyone squirm.

- Remember, toasts are meant to be tributes, not forums. Focus on the recipient(s) and reasons for this tribute. Don't ramble.

- Never use a toast to embarrass or deride. It will hit you like a boomerang.

- Feeling prepared helps calm nerves, so plan what you intend to say. There are many books on quotations and toasts to inspire. But be careful about memorizing a toast verbatim. If you blank out—and even experienced speakers do—you'll have nowhere to go. Instead, craft your toast from genuine sentiment supplemented by text. If the text evaporates in the moment, you still have something to say.

- Never read a toast.

- Raise your glass before making the toast, and then clink glasses with those around you before taking a sip. If you are in a large room full of people, simply lift the glass again in gesture when you finish speaking. Then take a sip.

- When others are making toasts, always raise your glass and take a sip at the conclusion. To not participate is rude.

For the sake of simplicity, we focus here on how to be a good host in one's own home. Hosting duties are not limited to that domain, however. You may host others in a restaurant, club, sports arena, banquet room, field, bus—almost anywhere. Any time you invite others to assemble, you are responsible for their having a good time. You are hosting.

The reason it is not necessary to delve into each of these scenarios individually is the basic principles of good hosting apply wherever you are. The good host anticipates his guests' every need. This requires forethought, planning, organization, and consideration. Like all social graces, it is the art of putting others at ease.

Between Chapter Three's instruction regarding the business lunch and the following points on entertaining at home, you should be able to extract all the basic tenets of good hosting. If not, we are sorely disappointed.

{ Tip: If you invite others to join you in a restaurant, private club, or other venue, make sure everyone will feel comfortable there. Inviting vegetarians to a famous steak house or those who might be offended by exclusive policies into a private club are not the acts of a considerate host. }

235

GIVING

SENDING INVITATIONS

For somewhat informal gatherings, it is equally acceptable to issue invitations by phone or mail. The former often gives you an immediate response; the latter ensures guests have the correct date, time, etc., written down. E-mail is acceptable only for the most casual gatherings among friends or colleagues.

Written invitations don't have to be fancy. The appropriate information penned on a plain white card is always acceptable.

Issue invitations two weeks in advance for a dinner party or special occasion like an anniversary celebration. One week in advance suffices for more casual get-togethers.

Don't issue invitations late in the week for the coming weekend unless you know your invitees very well. Last-minute invitations can be offensive, since they imply either the recipient's company is not in high demand or that he or she was not your first choice.

Make sure verbal and written invitations include the following information:

- Day of the week
- Date
- Time
- Address
- Attire (casual, coat and tie)
- Occasion when applicable (e.g., "Bon Voyage for Bonnie")
- Prompt for response (*RSVP, Please Reply,* or *Regrets Only*)
- Phone number for response
- Any instructions about parking or transportation

Note: If guests haven't responded to your invitation by two days before the party (*shame* on them!), it is appropriate to call and ask if they will be joining you.

CHECKLIST

Some people make entertaining at home look effortless. It isn't.

But it's not overwhelming if you make a checklist and stick to it every time.

Start this process at least a week before the party, more if it's a large gathering. You don't want nasty surprises the day before the event.

- **Determine the number of guests.** Take into consideration the size of your home, the number you can comfortably seat for dinner, parking, and expense. This may drive the kind of party you'll have. For example, if you want to invite the whole office, it may have to be just cocktails and hors d'oeuvre or beer and barbecue. If you can seat only six around the table for dinner, don't invite ten.

- **Plan and write out the menu.** Even if you are having it catered or using quality take-out, you still need to know the food. If it is a small gathering and limited menu, ask each guest if there is anything he or she prefers not to eat. This saves embarrassment for vegetarians and those with food allergies or restrictions. Don't forget to plan appetizers to set out and dessert. Be mindful of the capacities of your refrigerator, freezer, and oven, as well as eating and serving dishes. You don't want to plan for soup and discover you don't have enough bowls or wind up with a mountain of potato salad and no place to chill it.

- **Plan drinks.** (See "Tending the Bar," page 240.) Always have soda, water (sparkling and bottled), and juices for those not wanting alcohol. Decide where the bar will be set up and how people will get their drinks. Choose appropriate wines for dinner. In general, white wine goes with light-colored food like fish, seafood, chicken, and pastas with white sauces. Red wine accompanies red meats (beef, pork, lamb, buffalo, elk) and pastas with red sauces.

- **Make the grocery list.** Don't forget bread, butter, coffee, cream, sugar, artificial sweetener, lemons, limes, toilet paper, paper towels, and plenty of ice.

- **Check for correct number of plates, forks, glasses, wine glasses, and napkins.** Do you have enough steak knives? Do you have Champagne glasses if there will be toasts? Remember, you may need as many as three forks per person, depending on what you serve. Unless it is a big informal party for the whole gang, nix the paper plates and napkins and plastic glasses and cutlery. Use only the real stuff.

- **Do all shopping, set the table, and get out all serving dishes and utensils two to three days before the party.** Save the day of the party for more pressing matters. Like food preparation.

- **Clean the house the day before.** The whole house. People wander. And don't think you can cram everything into the hall closet and slam the door, because someone will inevitably mistake it for the bathroom.

- **Clean and spruce up bathrooms the day of the party.** You want them to sparkle. That's where guests spend time alone looking around. Make sure bathrooms are stocked with fresh soap, clean hand towels, and extra rolls of toilet paper. A lighted scented candle (preferably contained in glass so you don't burn down the house) and tissues are nice extras.

{TIPS}

If the hour approaches for guests to arrive and you are behind on preparations, drop everything to shower and dress. It is fine to set up the bar or finish making salad while guests are there. It's not fine to shower.

Not everyone is expected to be a wine connoisseur. There is nothing wrong with calling your local wine shop and asking for recommendations within your budget. These people are typically knowledgeable and happy to share that. Go over the menu and let him or her pick the wines. If you and your guests like their selection, write it down. You've made the first step toward becoming a connoisseur.

If you are not an experienced host, this is no time to get ambitious. The inexperienced cook trying to put on a gourmet dinner rarely succeeds. Ditto for trying to throw an upscale affair on a shoestring. Better to match both your experience and your budget. Everyone will be more comfortable.

Want to win a girl's heart? Cook her dinner. You don't have to be Emeril Lagasse to pull this off. In fact, the food doesn't even have to be good. It's the effort that counts. And no cheating with take-out, unless you make up for the shortcut with a spectacularly romantic presentation. As long as it's obvious you attempted to create a special meal, she will be flattered. If you happen to be a fabulous cook, she will be charmed.

Keep in mind not everyone loves dogs, cats, and/or children as much as you do. Unless it is a family affair or puppy party, kids should be otherwise occupied after making polite appearances, and pets should be sequestered.

Always remember good parties are less about perfect food and table settings and more about the atmosphere the host creates. As with everything in life, your attitude is infectious. Don't apologize for small spaces or a take-out menu. Instead, celebrate the evening and being together. If guests sense you're having fun, they will, too.

If dinner goes up in smoke (literally), have a good laugh at yourself and order pizza. It will make for a more fun, more memorable evening than if dinner had turned out as planned.

The best way to signal you don't want guests to smoke in your home is to remove all ashtrays.

TENDING THE BAR

- When stocking your home bar for company, buy quality ingredients like top brands of liquor. Ditto for mixers like fresh juice (not cheap reconstituted stuff) and good tonic. Always include a variety of appropriate garnishes like lemon and lime wedges and twists, olives for martinis, celery for bloody marys, and whatever else the beverage menu might require. Such attention to detail goes beyond expectation and speaks well of the host.

- Keep both red and white wine on hand. White wine should be served chilled (not with ice in it, but refrigerated). Red wine is always served at room temperature.

- Before guests arrive, open bottles of red and white wines or whatever your guests are likely to want. If the bottles are sealed, guests may feel awkward about requesting them.

- It's fine for the host to pour himself a glass of wine or beer or a cocktail before guests arrive. In fact, it can make them feel at ease about ordering when you say, "I've started with a glass of white wine, but I have red wine, cocktails, whatever you like." They will often follow the host's lead, so make sure you have enough of what you're drinking.

- It is nice if the host can make drinks for guests, but it is also acceptable for the busy host to show guests the bar and explain that everyone is making his or her own. This gives people something to do right away and helps generate conversation between arriving guests.

- Offering a special concoction at a party adds fun and a signature at the same time. A pitcher of margaritas, cosmopolitans, bloody marys, or some exotic cocktail you invent (assuming it's legal and tasty) can set the tone for the party. It can also be a money saver since it often keeps guests from downing more expensive fare.

- If you're trying to uncork a bottle of wine and the cork pops down into the bottle instead of out, you can do one of two things: take a long piece of string, tie a cork-size loop in it, lower it down around the cork, and pull it up and out (to *great* applause) OR leave the cork afloat. It won't hurt anything.

- If the bottle of wine is two years old (read the label) and its cork disintegrates upon opening, the wine is probably bad. If the wine is seventy years old and the cork disintegrates, the wine is probably very good. When faced with opening extremely old wines (lucky you), be extremely patient and careful.

- If bits of cork escape into your guests' glasses, no need to fish around with fingers. Instead, take a straw and capture each floating piece individually. Then cap the straw with your fingertip to create suction and draw the piece out.

The reason it is important to plan for and prepare as much food as possible before guests arrive is so you can devote yourself to seeing everyone is comfortable and has fun. That is the job of the host. Remember, you are there to serve, not be served.

...From the "hello"

Put the music on and finish preparing the bar at least thirty minutes before guests arrive. That way, the first guest will be assured of entering a party atmosphere.

Every guest should be warmly greeted and have a drink in hand within five minutes of arrival.

This doesn't sound too hard until you try to do it. If you have more than three guests, trying to answer the door, fix drinks, and engage everyone in conversation at once can prove indelicate at best. There's no perfect way to manage this alone.

{ Tip: You don't have to live in the Taj Mahal for guests to enjoy your home. In fact, it's better if you don't. Smaller spaces make people comfortable. Having fewer places to sit forces guests to move around and mingle, not sit down and settle into one conversation. }

Making Guests Feel A

The best solution is to have someone—a spouse, friend, or paid attendant—either open the door while you fill drink orders or vice versa.

If you don't have the luxury of help, greet the first guests at the door, show them to the bar, and start fixing them a drink. As other guests begin arriving, introduce them to one another and tell them you will be back for drink orders shortly or, if they like, they should feel free to get something for themselves. All bottles should be open, especially wine. Don't burden guests with difficult tasks.

The main thing is to not leave guests stranded with nothing to do and no one with whom to converse. It's no disaster if someone else opens the door and points out where coats go, but the host needs to provide the welcome and make introductions. Connecting guests frees you to greet newcomers. (See "Introductions," page 148.)

Mixing it up

Whether cocktails are before dinner or the main attraction, when people are drinking and mingling is the host's time to circulate. Be careful not to stay too long with one person or group, no matter how much you would like to. Spend time with everyone and be a catalyst for conversation between guests. Assuming you were paying attention in Chapter Three (page 148), each guest should know something about the other through your fine introductions.

If someone is standing or sitting alone, rush to the rescue. Invite him or her to come with you to see your collection of framed sports autographs, to hear another guest's tale about traveling, or, as a last resort, to help you do something like put ice in water glasses. All guests needs to feel their company is welcomed, even if it's by you in the kitchen.

Kitchen talk

Try not to sequester yourself in the kitchen for too long before dinner, abandoning your guests. Last-minute preparations are unavoidable, but lengthy exits are inexcusable.

Allowing guests in the kitchen as company while you work is up to you. People are naturally drawn to the comfort of kitchens, but they can take up critical physical and mental space while you're trying to work. Besides, if you are a messy cook, they may be better off not witnessing preparations. It's the old "watching sausage being made" thing.

There is no shame in shooing guests out of the kitchen if you need to be alone. Say something friendly like, "If you all wish to enjoy this dinner, I have to ask all of you to clear out. I'm not smart enough to think, talk, and cook at the same time."

{ Tip: You don't have to pay professional wages to get party help. Maybe you know a college student or someone else who would love to make extra money parking cars, serving, and/or cleaning up.

Pay at least $10 per hour if you want good help to come back again. You'll pay considerably more if the help is professional. }

Tip: Music sets the tone for a party. Choose it with your guests in mind. A dinner party focused on conversation calls for background music, preferably instrumental. Cocktails can use something livelier and a touch louder. But never force guests to yell over the music, unless dancing is the main attraction. In that case, remember to invite all your close neighbors before they invite the cops.

Tip: Good lighting is essential to good parties. No one looks good in a glare. Indirect lighting is best; overhead is worst. If you can't dim overhead lights, turn them off. Turn them off anyway if the room has lamps you can turn on instead. Turn on one lamp instead of three. Think romantic, unless this is a guy party. Then the glow of the television should suffice.

Candles provide warm light, they're cheap, and they disguise lots of decorating flaws. Use them alone or to supplement artificial light, and use as many as you can without making the place look like a sacrificial altar. By all means, don't place them where they can ignite flowers, furniture, fabric, or hair, and don't forget to extinguish every last one before bed.

Dinner may be served in one of three ways:

- Buffet, where food is set out for guests to serve themselves. Guests pick up plates, napkins, and silverware, or just plates if the table is set.
- Host puts food on the plates in the kitchen and presents them to guests.
- Host puts plates on the table and personally passes dishes to each seated guest (or has a waiter do this).

Note: The only food dish that belongs on the dining table is the bread basket. Putting serving dishes on the dining table for guests to pass among themselves boardinghouse-style is acceptable only at the most informal and friendly meals. Even so, keep in mind that hot dishes and all that picking up/putting down can scratch fine surfaces. Consider using a tablecloth or, better still, a buffet.

The most common order for serving courses is:

- Soup or appetizer
- Salad
- Entrée
- Dessert and coffee

In Europe, salad follows the entrée. You may do it this way if you are *really* that cosmopolitan.

SERVING RULES

- It is fine to put the first course (appetizer, soup, or salad) on the table and then summon guests.
- Serve guests to the left and clear dishes to the right.
- Wait until every guest is finished before clearing anyone's dish. Never hurry anyone to finish.
- Clear all the dishes for one course before serving the next. Never take more than two at a time, and do not stack dirty dishes.
- Courses should be served to each guest at the same time. In other words, one shouldn't be starting the entrée while another finishes salad.
- Be mindful of the table so you can clear dirty dishes as soon as is possible and polite. No one likes to stare at dirty plates.
- Have enough forks and spoons so none have to be reused. Never ask guests to retain a dirty utensil for the next course. If you must, collect utensils and, without fanfare, hand-wash quickly in soap and extra hot water. Replace on the table next to each place setting.

SERVING DINNER

{ Tip: The head of the table is usually reserved for the host, but a guest of honor or an elder family member may also be given that place. In any case, it's up to the host to give seating instructions. This can be done formally with a guest's name on a place card at each seat; informally at the beginning of the meal by telling guests where to sit; or generally, e.g., "Please take a seat. You are free to sit anywhere."

Although the last suggestion seems the most considerate, it may not be. If guests don't know one another well, they may feel awkward about where to sit and would appreciate place cards. Place cards also allow the host to mix it up, introduce people, and consider who would be good company for whom (and vice versa), thus orchestrating a successful evening. }

THE GRACIOUS DINNER PARTNER

- When the host or hostess signals it is time to sit down for dinner, do not dawdle. The food may be getting cold, which makes the one who prepared it anxious. That's inconsiderate.

- If there are place cards, find yours and stand at your chair. If there are none, wait for your host to assign seating. If he or she hasn't read this book and is saying nothing, politely ask where you should sit.

- The host should give instructions to be seated. Don't sit before the hostess or women at the table sit down. Assist the ones immediately around you with their chairs—not because you're stronger than they are but because you're nice.

- Put your napkin in your lap as soon as you sit down. (*For which one is yours and other mysteries of the place setting, see page 160.*)

- When the host picks up a fork to eat, that is your signal to begin. The host may also instruct you to start eating before he does. That is fine.

- Whether in a banquet hall, a restaurant, or someone's home, your main job as a dinner guest is to be attentive to those with whom you are seated. That means talking to the person seated to your

> { Tip: It is always appropriate and appreciated for a guest to propose a toast to the evening's host. It can be at the beginning or end, but in either case should honor the host's ability to create a great evening of food, fellowship, and friendship, or some combination thereof. }

right and your left (but *never* with food in your mouth). Don't turn your back on one for the duration of the evening while you converse with the other. Instead, alternate often. If this is going on all around the table, the conversation should keep flowing and no one should be idle. (*For tips on topics for conversation, see page 151.*) If it is an intimate gathering, there may be a single conversation involving the whole table with each guest contributing and, hopefully, no one guest monopolizing. If the group is thusly engaged, DO NOT initiate one-on-one conversations with those seated next to you. This is rude and disruptive. If your high school English teacher were there, she would ask you to come to the front of the room and share with the rest of the class what you had to say that was so important. We would applaud her.

- Eat your dinner. The food the host has put before you is a gift. If you do not accept it graciously and compliment it, the host will be disappointed at best, offended at worst. Non-eaters should not expect to be invited back.

- Offer to help the host clear dishes. If he or she declines your help, respect those wishes.

FRIENDLY REMINDERS FROM MOM:

- Keep your elbows off the table and close to your sides as you eat.

- Never talk with food in your mouth.

- Don't bite off more than you can chew.

- Keep your napkin in your lap, not tucked into your collar like a bib.

- Don't lean close to your plate and shovel your food. Sit up straight.

- Keep your mouth closed as you chew.

- Don't make any noise as you eat and drink. That includes humming.

- Don't play with your food.

THE BLACK TIE AFFAIR

Some guys get all nervous at the prospect of a formal black-tie dinner. Here's a news flash: The only difference is the suit.

The rules for a formal dinner are the same as for a civilized dinner in someone's home or a fine restaurant. Be confident about the place setting, basic table manners, and the few social courtesies written here, and you're a pro.

Now aren't you relieved?

DEAL KILLER LIGHTEN UP

It's poor form to dwell on business matters at a purely social function, even if the group consists of colleagues and clients. This is not the time and place.

DEAL KILLER SLOSHED

Regardless of what you've seen in the movies about the amiable inebriate, no one likes a drunk. To imbibe over several hours without exceeding personal limits, alternate every alcoholic drink with a nonalcoholic one, preferably water. Drink more water than wine at dinner, and be sure to eat whatever is available, even if it's only pretzels.

After The

If guests are having such a good time that they are reluctant to leave, good for you. You are a great host.

But it's not your obligation to sit up until 3:00 a.m. just because someone doesn't want to go home. In fact, it is best if you bring the evening to a close at its high point. That way, everyone goes home with good feelings.

There are a couple of ways to do this. One is to ask people to leave indirectly: "This has been a great evening. Too bad I have to get up early." Or, "I am so glad everyone was able to come this evening. I hope we can all get together again soon."

You can also start collecting glasses and tidying up. Guests often take that hint.

Do not, however, start washing dishes. This appears either too dismissive or like you expect help. Neither is a good way to end an evening.

{ Tip: When a guest brings a gift to a host, that gift is intended as thanks for the invitation. The host does not write a thank-you note for that gift. That would be thanking him for thanking him. It's a bit much. }

Party

Offers of "May I help?" are often polite and insincere. Guests usually relish an evening of someone else doing all the heavy lifting.

Do not expect them to help prepare, serve, or clear dishes between courses or at the end of the meal. You may ask them to do something easy and last-minute like light candles, but that's all.

The best tactic is to assure them you have everything handled and will summon help if needed. If one or more guests insist, or if it is a very informal gathering of good friends, accepting the help is not only acceptable, it is the gracious thing to do.

ENOUGH IS ENOUGH

The good host cannot be reluctant to tell an intoxicated guest, "Can I get you a soda or cup of coffee, Harry?" There is no need to be rude or critical, but do be firm. If Harry does not take the hint, hide his keys and call a cab. Lives and liability are at stake.

The considerate guest does not overstay his welcome. Be attentive to signals from the host—things like clearing dishes or statements such as, "Would you like this last bit of wine?" or "This has been great. I am sorry I have to get up early tomorrow."

Take your leave quickly with profuse thanks for being included. If it is a small gathering, be sure you also say good night to and shake hands with other guests, especially those you just met.

Follow up

The day after the party is the time to write your note of thanks. Don't be tempted to put it off. It may be forgotten or at least details will be fuzzier. The note need not be long, but should mention specific details about the evening (*"The lamb was just perfect"*).

Many people fail to follow up with thank-you notes for invitations. Those who do follow up ingratiate themselves.

The Party's Over

DEAL

DEAL KILLER
OENOPHILIA AND OTHER DISEASES

So you are well versed in the rich subtleties of fine food or wine? Well, good for you. Now do the rest of us a favor and cork it.

Such lofty education may enhance your own culinary enjoyment, but it rarely does the same for listeners. Instead, it smacks of elitism and resonates as pompous. Save the soliloquies on the '81 versus '83 Cabernets and the ecstasy of white truffles for WFSC (Wine and Food Snob Club). Your erudite views are unwelcome around most tables, especially when your level of sophistication might make a host feel inadequate.

DEAL KILLER
IT'S NOT MUSICAL CHAIRS

Never bring an uninvited guest to a social event. This sounds like a no-brainer, but plenty of people exhibit no brains in this regard.

It's this simple: If the host is providing food and/or drink, it's inconsiderate to expect him to feed and entertain anyone he didn't invite.

If your fun-loving cousin Larry will be visiting from San Francisco the weekend you've been invited to a friend's party, explain the situation to your friend. He or she will either say, "Bring Larry along." Or, "We'll catch you next time." Asking is fine. Surprising the host is not.

The worst sort of inconsideration is to bring an uninvited guest to a seated dinner. Your guest could well wind up without a seat, much to the embarrassment of all. Never do that to your host or guest.

If the invitation is addressed to you only—be it a formal wedding or a backyard barbecue—don't assume you may bring a guest. If you wish to bring a date or spouse (preferably not both), call to ask the host's permission.

Besides the rude factor, another good reason never to bring uninvited guests is those guests may be uninvited for good reasons. Unwittingly, you might bring someone who is at odds with the host or another guest, ruining everyone's evening. If he or she is announced ahead of time, sticky situations can be avoided.

Hosting houseguests is much the same
as hosting a party: Your primary concern
is creating a comfortable atmosphere for
them. Because they are staying over,
however, there are a few extra details
you must mind.

Hosting house

Before houseguests arrive, do the following:

- Establish exact times of your guest's arrival and departure, as well as means of transportation, so there is no one left standing on doorsteps or in train stations.

- Talk to them beforehand about any planned activities and what weather to expect so they can pack accordingly.

- Ask if there is anything special they would like to do so you can buy tickets, make sure attractions are open, etc. But don't expect them to be full of ideas if they've never visited in your city. It's your responsibility as host to come up with suggestions for entertainment they might like.

- Inform them if you have pets. Some people are allergic to dogs or cats or simply have no desire to cohabitate with them, even for one evening. Either recommend a nearby hotel or board Fido and Kitty.

- Ask if guests have any dietary restrictions, special requests, or drink preferences (diet or regular soda?). Ask what they like for breakfast (coffee? tea? cream? artificial sweetener? juice? bacon and eggs? granola?). Stock their requests along with some easy snack foods and bottled water.

- Clean the guest sleeping quarters and put clean sheets on the guest bed just before they arrive. Lay out fresh towels on the bed for each guest.

- Make sure the bathroom they'll be using is immaculate. Include an ample supply of toilet paper and soap. It's also nice to have a fresh toothbrush, toothpaste, deodorant, and disposable razor in case the guests forget any of these necessities.

"Houseguests are like fish. After three days, both begin to smell."—W. C. Fields

PLANNING

guests

The Welcome House

ed guest

Many of the tenets of a good guest apply to the houseguest. There are a few more considerations, however.

- Clean up after yourself. This applies even if you and/or your host aren't particularly tidy. Try harder. Make your bed each morning (if you can't effect the perfectly folded corner, at least spread up the bedspread) and hang up to dry all towels you use. Keep toiletries in your room, not spread out on the bathroom sink, unless no one shares your bath. Put dirty dishes in the sink or dishwasher.
- If your host cooks, offer to help clean up.
- Respect household sleeping routines. Early risers should be quiet until the rest of the house gets up.
- Offer to pay for meals eaten out. You may split some, but make sure at least one is your treat.
- Be kind and attentive to all household members.
- Give hosts some space and time to themselves. Don't expect them to be on call for you 24/7.
- Bring a gift with you (flowers, wine, a book, nonperishable food) and send a gift along with the thank-you note within a week of returning home.

DEAL KILLER
NO SMOKING

Don't smoke inside someone's house without asking permission. If you must smoke, ask the host for the best place to step outside. Dispose of the evidence afterwards.

DEAL KILLER
WHERE'S WALDO?

We toss tardiness and the dreaded no-show in the same ugly barrel here, because both represent transgressions of absenteeism and throw the host's schedule into pandemonium.

Being late is not such a crime provided the tardiness is minimal. In fact, we recommend arriving between ten and fifteen minutes after the invitation's stated start time to give the host a few grace minutes. Beyond fifteen minutes, however, people begin to wonder of your whereabouts or whether you're coming at all. That forces the host to push cooking and serving schedules back and generally stresses the party.

Bottom line: Be on time. If for some reason you can't, call. It's that simple.

The second part of this—the no-show—is so offensive, we will not even dignify it with explanation. Pull one of these for a social occasion—especially a small event—and it will never be forgotten.

That said, there are times when circumstances prevent you from attending. In that case, call as soon as you realize you won't be there. If calling is not possible—it's a large reception on a remote island—call with regrets as soon as possible. Leave a message for the host to receive when he or she gets back in cell phone range or call the next day to express your regrets.

DURING

- When guests arrive, first show them to their room. Then offer a brief tour of the house so they'll feel at home. Point out any household quirks they need to know. Not as in chipped paint and squeaky floors. As in backwards hot and cold water handles in the shower or hidden light switches. Show them where you keep drinking glasses, drinks, and snacks. Urge them to help themselves.

- Ask guests what time they expect to get up in the morning and if they need an alarm. Honor their sleeping habits, even if they don't complement yours. Keep the noise down.

- The best host gets up before his guests. But if that's not in the cards, before going to bed, set out coffee, tea, and any breakfast items that don't need refrigeration. Set the coffeemaker timer to brew automatically. Make sure guests know to help themselves.

- Ask guests if there is anything they need.

- Don't overschedule, for everyone's sake. Allow some down time and respect a guest's right to privacy. If he or she wants to spend time alone reading, don't take it personally.

- Don't feel obligated to cook if you can't, but it's nice to share at least one meal besides breakfast

- Nor should you pay for every meal eaten in restaurants. When eating out, suggest the bill be split or say something like, "I'll get this one. You get the next." Only the most inconsiderate guest will ignore the hint. And only the most inconsiderate host would pick up the breakfast tab at Waffle House and expect his guests to then cover dinner at Four Seasons. C'mon, guys.

- If you have a prior commitment or routines like a standing Saturday tennis game, invite guests to come along. If that's not possible or they decline, you can still go, provided you're back in two hours or less. A Saturday golf game that excludes guests

The Good Guest

Everyone would like to be the celebrated guest, the man whose answering machine blinks incessantly with messages of invitation. Dinners at fine restaurants, weekends at the beach, rounds of golf at Augusta, ski vacations at a friend's private lodge: Oh, for such opportunities simply because we are blessed with splendid wit, good humor, dashing looks, and a clever tongue.

If that does not fully describe you, don't despair. For the social life we envision, most of us must resort to playing the one card we are all dealt: the ability to be the kind, thoughtful, likeable, easy guest.

It's much the same principle as hosting, really. Mind a few details, follow some basic rules, and enjoy yourself.

DEAL KILLER COMMUNICATION BREAKDOWN

When someone is tailoring her schedule around you, as is the case for any host expecting a guest, it is essential that a guest communicate. Whether you are dinner guest or houseguest, if there is the slightest alteration in your arrival or departure time or any other plans for the visit, you must tell your host immediately. Surprises, last minute "oh-by-the-way" comments, and, worst of all, failure to notify the host of those changes are deadly rude.

{ Tip: BUSINESS AS USUAL When you are invited to the boss's house for dinner or to a big client's country club for a round of golf, make no mistake: This is still business. This is not the time to let your hair down, have a few drinks, slap the guys on the back, and tell sketchy jokes. Nor is it an opportunity to gossip about others in your corporation, betray confidences, or give frank opinions you would never share in the office. It may feel like an outing "among friends," but it is instead a "friendly outing." There's a big difference. Have a good time, but respect the boundaries. }

{ Tip: YOU, TOO? One thing to remember as you arrive at the cocktail party or dinner, formal reception, or informal tailgate gathering: All guests feel some level of insecurity. No matter how comfortable everyone else appears or how intimidating certain people are, rest assured they're human, too. You may think you can't talk to so-and-so with the perfectly tailored suit and gray hair, but you may find he would welcome your company. You may find you're both closet NASCAR fans and become friends for life.

All this is to say it's OK if you feel awkward as a guest in social situations. Everyone does. }

PLANNING THE PARTY

- Always bring the host a small gift to offer as soon as you arrive. Wine or spirits make good choices, so long as you don't expect the bottle to be opened at the party. A fragrant candle, gourmet flavored oil or vinegar, or some other high-end nonperishable food/beverage item is also acceptable, as is a book that reflects the host's interests or hobby or a music CD you're certain the host would like. Flowers are lovely, but they often mean the hostess has to stop everything, find a vase, trim stems, and add water. Still, better flowers than empty-handed.

- When replying to an invitation by phone, ask if there is anything you can bring. If they say "wine," ask what color. In this case, no other gift is necessary.

- When the dress code is ambiguous, dressing up is preferable to dressing down. In other words, better to show up in an unnecessary tie than to be the only one wearing shorts. Besides, dressing up shows respect for the host.

{ Tip: When a host insists that you "make yourself at home," this doesn't mean you can open drawers and cabinets, put your feet on the furniture, or rifle through the CD collection. It's a figure of speech. As a considerate party guest, a good rule of thumb is to refrain from doing anything you wouldn't do in the boss's office with him or her watching, dancing and drinking being the exceptions. }

KILLER
DEAL OFF LIMITS

Whether party guest or houseguest, unless your host urges you to explore the house, don't. Some hosts take pride in their environment and enjoy sharing it; others prefer that the rest of the house remain private.

KILLER
DEAL DOUBLE DIPPING

The full spectrum of social eating today requires dipping: French baguette in herbed olive oil, fresh veggies in yogurt dressing, Tostitos in microwave cheese stuff. A rule to remember: *Never* double dip. After the bread/veggie/chip has touched your lips, it does not go back in the communal dip. If you must optimize your dipper, break it in half before dipping or spoon a small amount of dip onto your plate.

- If it is a large gathering, find the host immediately and say hello.

- Move right into the crowd or group and, if there are those to whom you haven't been introduced, introduce yourself. Ask how he or she knows the host. It's always a good opener.

- Gravitate toward the middle of the room instead of hanging around the bar or food table. It's more sociable.

- Hold your drink in your left hand so your right hand won't be cold and clammy for handshakes.

- Don't corner people. Always leave space for someone to graciously move away into another conversation.

- If there is a celebrity or VIP executive in the group, it is fine to approach and introduce yourself or say hello. But do not monopolize this individual. Sucking up is never attractive.

- Spend only five or ten minutes with any one person before moving on. The point of cocktails is to mingle.

- We are all guilty of finding friends or acquaintances in a crowd and sticking with them. No matter how insecure you feel, force yourself to move around.

- If someone approaches the group or person with whom you are talking, acknowledge and include him or her immediately. Make introductions if necessary. If you are in the middle of a topic, tell the newcomer what you are talking about.

- Be a real hero. If you see someone who looks alone or uncomfortable, come to the rescue with conversation.

- Holding a plate of food and a drink while standing leaves no free hand for eating or shaking hands. Find a place to set your drink nearby, and then get food. Overloading your plate is asking for trouble. Better not to eat than to attempt such a balancing act.

- At some point during the party, ask the host if there is anything you can do to help out. This is especially nice if the cocktail party precedes dinner. The host may be looking for someone to fill water glasses or light candles, but may be reluctant to ask.

OMING

www.tomjames.com

Even though it shouldn't be this way, people have a tendency to judge us by our appearance.

Think that's an overstatement? Revisit a video clip of the first televised presidential debates in 1960 between Richard M. Nixon and John F. Kennedy. The black-and-white camera showed America an impeccably groomed, attractive Kennedy. Afterwards, polls confirmed that Nixon won the debate in the minds of the radio listeners and Kennedy won hands down with the TV audience. Appearance was more important than content. Some say the camera won Kennedy the election.

You may have lesser things at stake, but why ignore an obvious advantage?

Besides, let's not overlook the fact nothing repels the opposite sex like neglect of personal hygiene. This is another reason to pay attention to grooming. A body well cared for is a body sensual.

Not vanity, just good sense. Not narcissism, just confidence.

Grooming embraces details. If you're a bigger-picture kind of guy, no sweat. Understand how imperative good grooming is and incorporate a few essentials into a simple routine. Pretty soon these details will become second nature. A few good habits, that's all.

Since this book is about getting to the top, let's start there.

Hair

It's often said a good haircut is as important as a good suit. We concur. If you want to make the wrong kind of lasting impression, bad hair tops the list.

For men's hair—and all other aspects of a man's appearance, for that matter—one basic rule applies: Nothing about it should stand out—or, in this case, up. The optimum male look should be a total package without singular distraction. Bad hair can definitely provide singular distraction.

Good advice? Seek professional help.

The fellow who has been cutting your hair at the corner barbershop for $10 a clip since you were five may be a good buddy and fine technician, but what you need at this moment is a seasoned stylist. Someone who can analyze your hair, face, body build, and lifestyle and execute the perfect cut to suit your professional image. This is the difference between a $10 haircut and a $40 haircut. There is a difference. Trust us; others notice.

But that doesn't mean you have to be totally at the stylist's mercy. First, you should be sitting in his or her chair because someone whose hair you admire sent you. Ask around for recommendations. In case you haven't noticed, people are full of advice and more than willing to share it.

The style you want is short, neat, and current but not trendy. This cut requires little time when getting ready, keeps its composure, and looks professional.

Before you go for the appointment, flip through magazines and find a style you like. Consider it a guideline only, because the texture and thickness of your hair may not work in that exact cut. Show the photo to the stylist anyway. A picture is worth a thousand words, maybe more when it comes to the average man describing a hairstyle.

{Tip: Some men's hair grows slowly, some fast, some not at all. On average, the short hairstyle you want needs a trim every three to four weeks to maintain its composure. Don't trust your eye or memory. At the end of every cut, make an appointment for the next one.}

WHAT'S WHAT

SCULPTING LOTION: Good for giving fine hair texture. Also use to smooth down frizzy hair.

POMADE: Good for medium to coarse hair to style a short cut. Use sparingly. Has a petroleum base.

MOUSSE: Good for making thinner hair look thicker. Mousse is the application exception because a quarter-size dollop goes on wetter hair. Always apply to the root, not the hair shaft itself.

GEL: Good on sleeker styles. High-holding gel resembles clear glue in consistency and result. Soft-holding gel is less tenacious and keeps wet hair looking that way. (This is especially useful if you want the office guessing whether you lunched with a prospective client or at the gym.)

TONIC: Good for mild hold and to refresh the scalp. Usually greaseless, this classic men's hair product can still make hair look oily. Think Humphrey Bogart and Fred Astaire.

HAIR SPRAY: Light-hold hair spray is good for taming wavy, curly, or frizzy hair against humidity without a lacquered look. High-hold spray comes in a pump and will basically stop a fly in mid-air. Think news anchors and televangelists.

GLOSSING WAX: Good for adding shine without hold. Use sparingly.

HAIR PRODUCTS

If you remember only one thing about hair products, let it be this:

A LITTLE DAB WILL DEFINITELY DO YA.

Applying too much is a common mistake men make with hair products. You never want your hair to look plastered, stiff, or otherwise untouchable. A controlled, natural look is the object. Put a dime-size application in your palm, rub hands together, and apply to thoroughly towel-dried, not wet, hair. Comb it through, style, and let dry.

The competent stylist can adapt the style to best suit the thickness, wave, curl, and/or growth pattern of your hair. A good cut is your best defense against wiry, coarse, fine, straight, or any of the many adjectives applicable to human hair. Forget trying to straighten, curl, or otherwise reverse your hair's natural tendencies. It rarely works. A well-executed cut does work.

The stylist should also be your navigator through the confusing and sometimes frightening world of hair products. He or she can prescribe the right shampoo and conditioner for the health of your hair, as well as any styling aids. (See sidebar.) Keep sideburns trimmed between haircuts, preferably with an electric razor specially equipped to do the job.

{Tip: Make sure the hairstylist cleanly shaves the back of your neck. Hair on the neck not only looks bad, it also causes problems. Men prone to ingrown hairs in this area might consider having it removed with wax (it hurts for a split second, but lasts several weeks) or by laser, which kills the hair follicle permanently.}

Hair loss

Men's sensitivity about their hair, or more aptly lack thereof, has prompted a whole host of woeful attempts at replacement and/or disguise. The results are akin to the face-lift: If it's done well, no one ever knows. If it's not done well, everyone knows.

Should your method for hiding natural hair deficiencies fall in the latter category, understand that such blatant attempts at fooling the public inevitably diminish a man's dignity. This applies not only to hair follies, but also to bad tans from a bottle, gleaming white choppers, and obvious undergarments designed to give shape where there is none.

Attempts at illusion to correct nature carry sizeable risks. This is not the time to be brave.

Besides, no one cares nearly as much about your hair loss as you do. Get over yourself. Forget toupees, plugs, and comb-overs. If your hair begins to thin out, you are far better off cutting it close to the scalp. This minimizes the loss visually and looks good generally. The modern eye has come to appreciate a balding or bald head in old and young men alike. Keep the rest of the body in shape, and disappearing hair will disappear from impact. Think Bruce Willis, Sean Connery, Michael Jordan.

If you choose to impede natural hair loss, there are few tested regimes that can get results.

Minoxidil applied topically and DHT inhibitors taken internally are two possibilities. The former can be found over-the-counter in Rogaine, but the latter requires a prescription. Both require long-term commitment. Consult a dermatologist.

Color

Hair color has come a long way since black shoe polish on the temples to disguise the gray. Much of what we see now done by professional stylists looks lovely. *On women.*

But hair color for men is still iffy business. Distinctive highlights may be all the rage, but they can fall into the same category as comb-overs and other faux pas: unnecessary distraction. It smacks of too much time spent in front of the mirror, too little time spent on more worthy endeavors. Not a good idea.

Gray highlights are something else entirely, as long as they are perfectly natural.

Attempts to cover up graying hair rarely look as good as the transition or succeed in subtracting years. Some attempts do succeed in making the wearer look insecure and foolish. A nice head of well-kept, well-cut gray hair, on the other hand, makes a man appear distinguished and experienced. Revel in it.

DEAL KILLER
NO ONE LIKES A FLAKE

One positive from all those inane commercials depicting people humiliated by dandruff is most men have noted and conquered this grooming problem. If you're not among them, you need to be. Dandruff makes you look unclean and oblivious, neither of which is desirable in love or work.

Most men think dandruff signals overly dry scalp and immediately run for a drugstore dandruff shampoo. In reality, dandruff is excess cell turnover that can signal dry or oily conditions. Not knowing which you have can make things worse.

First, get a proper diagnosis from a knowledgeable stylist or dermatologist. If the problem is too much oil, use a shampoo with zinc pyrithione. If the problem is dryness, a tar-based or selsun-based shampoo works best.

Beware of the drugstore-variety remedies that contain high alkaline levels. The acidity can be harsh on the hair.

Stay on dandruff shampoo for thirty days, and then rotate off. Don't use it indefinitely. If the problem recurs, retreat for thirty days.

You've been shampooing your own hair since you were old enough to shower. Think you know what you're doing?

Maybe. Maybe not.

In either case, a few tips won't hurt.

- Never use bar soap to wash your hair. (If you've been backpacking for twelve days without bathing, make an exception.)

- Ditch the drugstore shampoo. Much of it is too alkaline, which, by stripping hair of its natural oil, causes hair to produce too much oil as compensation. The result is dandruff or unhealthy hair. Consult a stylist for a pH-balanced, salon-quality shampoo matched to individual hair texture. Think economy car vs. performance car: better stuff, better results.

- Wash your hair every day? Only if it's very oily. Otherwise, skip a day occasionally and just rinse with water. Too much shampooing dries hair and causes it to lose luster.

- Alternate shampoos. Either use two and switch every other day, or use one for a couple of weeks, then switch to another, and so on. Hair is like muscle: Both get used to repetition and eventually stop responding as well.

- Lather, rinse, repeat is one of the great marketing scams of all time. Once is plenty.

- Pour a quarter-size amount of shampoo on your fingers. Rub your hands together to spread the shampoo; then use your fingertips—not flat palms—to apply it to your scalp. Massage into your scalp and hairline to remove oil from the surrounding skin. Don't rub too hard. Wet hair is vulnerable. Rinsing gets enough shampoo through the hair shaft to cleanse it.

- Use a conditioner. Two-in-one shampoos don't count. Conditioner goes on the hair shaft, not on the scalp. Thick hair needs a quarter-size conditioner application; thin hair, dime-size. If your hair is extra dry, leave conditioner on for thirty minutes occasionally as therapy. Rinse.

- Very hot water is hard on your hair and body. It may feel great, but it wreaks havoc on a daily basis. Rinsing hair with lukewarm water is better. Cold is best for a final rinse, as it contracts hair for styling.

- Towel-dry gently. Apply any hair product. Comb your hair into place using a comb that is half widely spaced teeth, half fine teeth. The wide teeth pull through thicker parts of the hair; the fine teeth provide finish and control, especially around closer-cropped sections.

- Once styled, allow the hair to dry naturally. Use a blow dryer only if fine hair needs volume. To add volume, brush the hair with a vent brush in the opposite direction from how you would style it and aim warm air at the roots (low heat, low setting). When it's dry, gently comb or brush it into place.

Facial Hair

{ Tip: Stop the bleeding

A tiny bit of toilet paper placed strategically over a shaving nick might stem the flow, but what happens when you forget it's there and head out to an important meeting? Nothing like looking inept, goofy, and gross all at once.

Purchase a styptic pencil. It does the same thing without those unpleasant side effects. }

If you have facial hair, keep it closely manicured. No bushy beards, no straggly moustache hairs. Have the appropriate tools (fine-point barber scissors, fine-tooth comb, razor) and use them frequently. Shampoo them along with your hair.

The only career where oddly carved beards and handlebar moustaches are acceptable is that of biker. It may be fun, but usually doesn't pay well.

According to Braun, maker of electric shavers, the average man shaves
the length of an eighteen-hole golf course every eighteen months.
No wonder the male face can feel like a sand trap.
A few tips to keep you out of the rough.

- Shave in the shower or immediately afterwards. The steam opens pores and
  makes skin more pliable, but don't fry yourself. Warm water works as well
  and doesn't dehydrate the skin.
- If you're not showering, wet a washcloth with very hot water, wring it out,
  drape it over your face for a few minutes (like people flying first class
  internationally do, courtesy of the nice flight attendant), and then shave.
- Apply shaving cream or gel liberally and let it soften your beard for at least
  a minute before shaving. Spend a few bucks for a salon-quality product.
  Your skin will reward you.
- Shave in the direction that the hair grows. In general, that's a downward
  stroke. Upward strokes can cause razor bumps and ingrown hairs.
- Apply gentle pressure. No digging. Make strokes short, even, and quick
  but controlled. Rinse the blade between strokes.
- Pay special attention under the nostrils and lower lip and in front of the
  ears. These spots are often missed and/or nicked.
- Alcohol and shaving don't mix. Alcohol-based foams and aftershaves
  dry the skin. (And cocktails make you clumsy.)
- Change a razor blade every week or two, more often if your beard is heavy.
  An overused blade tugs at hair instead of cutting through cleanly. You'll
  know when it's time.

SHAVING

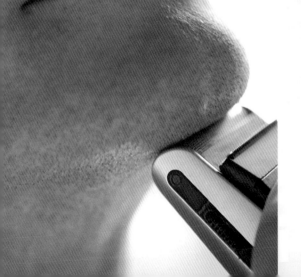

Electric razors have come a long way, but they're still less bang for lots more bucks: i.e., the
shave is not as close and the drag is harder on the skin than a standard wet shave.

But, they can save time and face. Own a good one for a late-afternoon/pre-evening
touchup or a Saturday morning quickie and for ultimate portability. Keep it in your briefcase.

If you use an electric razor for more than the occasional shave, consider one that can
be used wet. The warm water (or even better, steam from the shower) softens the beard,
making it less resistant to the razor's pull.

DEAL KILLER
BUSHY NOSE AND EAR HAIR

Never noticed you have them? Chances are someone else has.

These are two areas you must not neglect. Outcroppings can destroy an otherwise polished look.

For nose hair, buy a battery-powered nose-hair trimmer. It costs about $10 and is available at most pharmacies. Stick it in each nostril once a week, but no farther than the mirror sees (this is not sinus surgery). The sensation tickles, no worse. Plucking is far more painful and not recommended. Trimming with round-tipped scissors is another option, but more tedious and not as thorough.

Some nose-hair trimmers also work on ear hair. The little round-tipped scissors and a good mirror (better still, a good friend) are the sure thing. Some guys have ear hair waxed by professionals, but it's not wise. The skin in the ears is very delicate. The hot wax and pulling can tear tissue and cause problems far worse than ear hair.

Eyebrows: One is never enough

The biggest offense in men's eyebrows is the dreaded monobrow: eyebrows that bridge into one continuous line for that lovely Cro-Magnon look. Fix this, but not by shaving in between brows. Shaving anywhere around brows is asking for major league trouble. Plucking or waxing, preferably by a professional aesthetician, provides the easy solution to this unsightly distraction.

Most men think heavy eyebrows are sexy. They would be right and wrong.

Strong eyebrows frame and enhance eyes, thereby adding appeal.

But lush eyebrows and uncontrolled eyebrows are two different things. The former is sexy; the latter is decidedly not.

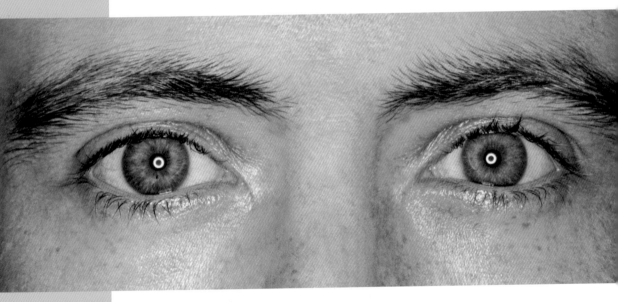

Eyebrows can be shaped several ways to look perfectly natural and, yes, sexy. One is by tweezing those few stray hairs that grow well outside the thickest part of the brow, especially down toward the outer corners of the eyes. Also pluck stray hairs that grow too long to lie with the rest, the ones that look like bug antennae. Be careful to grab only one hair at a time. Do it after a shower when pores are open, and tug in the direction the hair grows.

Many professional hairdressers and aestheticians (available at salons and spas) can do this for you. For a more long-term solution, they can also wax around the brow. This consists of applying a warm wax to the area, letting it cool, and peeling it off quickly, taking hair follicles with it. It smarts (like ripping athletic tape off your hairy leg), but the results are cleaner and last about six weeks. If you can't bear the thought of a repeat treatment, at least you now have a template for tweezing.

Mouth

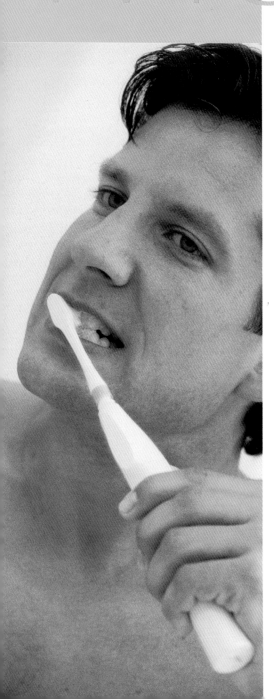

This entire section on oral hygiene could be labeled a "deal killer" because infractions can be devastating. The eyes may be the window to the soul, but the mouth is the PA system. So much of who we are and what we do draws attention to our mouths. People notice our mouths as they contemplate message, motive, masculinity. There is no bigger turnoff in business and romance than cracked lips, bad breath, and unsightly teeth.

There's no excuse for these, either.

Whiteners

Yellow teeth are one of the key elements that make you look old. Fortunately, they are so easy to remedy these days.

Whiteners are everywhere, and some are much better than others. As with so many things, you get what you pay for. Whitening toothpastes and over-the-counter bleaching products are relatively inexpensive and may result in lightening a shade or two. Dentist-supervised or in-office bleaching can lighten teeth three to eight shades, but the cost is somewhere between $300 and $1,000.

For real results, consult a dentist about one of several professional whitening methods available. One method is done at home with custom-made trays filled with a bleaching solution worn nightly for two to four weeks. Another is an in-office application of a stronger solution aided by a special light, heat, and/or laser. This only takes an hour, with a few return sessions as needed.

It's all painless and worth the extra money spent for a more compelling smile.

Orthodontia

Crooked teeth and pronounced overbites are not only cosmetic drawbacks; they can also present significant health woes if not treated.

Depending on the specific problem, alignment and bite challenges don't necessarily mean two years with a mouth full of metal. Innovations in orthodontia now offer attractive alternatives like clear plastic trays that fit over your teeth and correct gently. Other people can't even see them. Expensive, but well worth it.

If you suspect a problem, book a visit to the orthodontist. You're doing yourself a lifelong favor, not to mention those who have to look at you.

Breath

Religously following all the cleaning steps above is Job #1. Job #2 is to carry tiny, potent breath mints (never gum) at all times and pop them frequently and discreetly. Chewing a bite of parsley (that delicate green stuff on your plate for decoration) after a meal, again discreetly, also freshens the breath.

Although most bad breath results from bacteria in the mouth, it can also stem from sinus problems, infection, gum disease, diabetes, kidney failure, liver malfunction, stress, dieting, snoring, and/or hormonal changes. If yours is chronic, see a doctor and get to the source.

- Brush and floss twice per day with a mint toothpaste.
- Brush your tongue and inside cheeks with a little toothpaste. They harbor smelly bacteria, too.
- Rinse and gargle with mouthwash.
- Have your teeth cleaned professionally every four to six months or every three months if you smoke or drink a lot of coffee, tea, or red wine.
- Don't put off necessary dental work, like fillings.

Lips

Lip balm is not lipstick. You can—and should—use it without feeling girly. It moisturizes lips and, provided it has an SPF of 15 or better, protects them from sun and wind. Just don't apply it in public, please. Choose one without fragrance and don't use so much that your lips appear greasy. That's almost as bad as dry, cracked, and peeling, which is what you're trying to avoid.

DEAL KILLER DADGUMIT

Your mother was right. Chewing gum makes you look positively bovine. It lowers your IQ the minute it hits your mouth.

If you are concerned about your breath (and you should be), carry strong breath mints.

The only time gum is permissible is in flight and only if the pressure bothers your ears. In that case, chew discreetly during takeoff and landing and spare your hapless seatmates the rest of the time.

DEAL KILLER OPEN FOR BUSINESS

Speaking of mouths, yours should remain closed in public unless you're talking (and not eating), laughing, or kissing. Never open it while there is food in it. Never breathe through it. Never allow it to open while listening, walking, sitting, etc. This makes you look simple.

Some men allow the orifice to gape without knowing it, especially while eating. Ask a close friend for candid feedback. Take a plate of food into your own bathroom and watch yourself in the mirror while you eat. Closed mouth means just that: no slightly parted lips, no intermittent lax jaw to move food around. It's disgusting.

CLEANSING & MOISTURIZING

- Drink lots of water. This hydrates the skin and aids elimination and practically every other aspect of a sound body.

- Wash your face and body with warm water. Hot water robs skin of its natural moisturizing oils.

- Deodorant soaps are good for destroying the bacteria that cause bodily odor, but they can be hard on skin, especially the face. Wash your face with a milder pH-balanced facial cleanser or glycerin-based soap. Rinse thoroughly.

- About once a week, use a gentle exfoliating scrub on your face. This is a grainy cream or gel that removes dead surface skin cells so impurities aren't trapped in pores. It can help prevent occasional pimples (not to be confused with acne, which requires other measures) and ingrown hairs. It makes skin look more vibrant.

- For feel-good skin that looks polished and healthy, use an exfoliating scrub all over occasionally.

- Apply face and body lotions immediately after your shower (and a quick towel-dry) to trap moisture. Applying lotion after skin dries is much less effective.

Skin Care

Saving Face

Up until a few years ago, the term "skin care" was not in the male vocabulary. But the ravages of ultraviolet rays, harsh environments, and the stress of everyday living have made it not only acceptable, but smart.

We're not advocating melon-chiffon facials at the local spa, (although once you tried it, you would be hooked). We are advocating a few sensible strategies for saving the only skin you have. You will look healthier and more vigorous.

Cleansing and hydration are key. Aged, leathery faces are dehydration revealed. Add moisture and the aging process slows.

Tanning

Used to be a man's tan signified leisure time on golf courses and beaches, good health, and riches. Sun-summoned pigment still holds some of that mystique, even though we now know any change in pigment signifies damage and increased risk of skin cancer.

All is not lost, however. Just be smart. Smart is never going out in the sun without SPF 15 protection or higher on exposed parts. Smart is an invisible daily moisturizer with SPF 15 applied to the face and hands every morning. Smart is a hat on the golf course and avoidance of tanning salons entirely.

{ Tip: There are distinct differences between face and body lotions. Own both and don't use them interchangeably.

Quality is key for face moisturizer; quantity is important for body lotion. Spend money on a good men's face moisturizer compatible with your skin type. Consult a dermatologist, aesthetician, or at least a trained men's skin-care salesperson. Use daily on face and neck after cleansing.

You can get by with a reputable drugstore body lotion, but don't buy the cheapest available. Pick one of reasonable substance and apply generously over the body after your shower. }

Even smarter is
salon-applied spray-on tan, if you
must go bronze. Sounds hokey, but no
harmful UVs and it looks closest to natural
of the alternatives.

Beware home-tanning products and
bronzers. Some are convincing, but many can turn
orange and/or look extremely artificial. Then
you're in the category with comb-overs.

The smartest of all is to forgo the tan.
Work on having healthy, vibrant skin instead.
That, too, is very, very sexy.

DEAL KILLER TATTOOS

Body art may have transcended Hell's Angels to gain some measure of acceptability throughout polite society, but it still does nothing for the professional image. The business world is not impressed that one night on college spring break your walk on the wild side resulted in a nasty case of amnesia and an artful tattoo of a two-headed snake.

Keep tattoos covered and no harm done. Even better: Consult a dermatologist about removal.

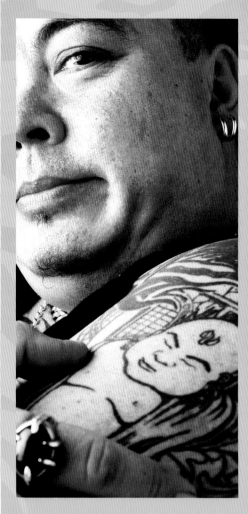

DEAL KILLER
THE NOSE KNOWS

Just as one must perfect the delicate balance in so many aspects of life, so it is with fragrance. For men, this means smelling neither too sweet nor too sour.

Unfortunately, many men seem oblivious to this personal offense. Take note.

Better still, take precautions. Bathe daily with a deodorant soap. Follow with a deodorant to mask odor or an antiperspirant to both mask odor and impede moisture. For many, this suffices.

If you wish to indulge in aftershave or cologne, fine, but know the difference and beware the quality and application. Aftershave can be used in the morning, but always with a light touch. Drop a dime's worth in the palm, rub palms together, and gently pat on the shaved areas.

Cologne is only for social occasions. Inexpensive varieties are out, with the exception of classic Old Spice. Select one from a fine men's store or department store by trying it on. Never test more than three in one visit. The nose loses track.

Remember, wearing too much fragrance is as offensive as body odor. Cologne is not aftershave. Don't pour it in your hand and slap it on your face. Don't spray it on your face, either. Apply to clean skin only (not as a cover-up when you really need a shower), and spray lightly once or twice on chest, neck, or forearms—not all three.

If you have cologne or aftershave on your hands, wash them immediately. Some people are allergic to any fragrance and will be allergic to you if you transfer it in a handshake or through the air after overzealous application.

Rule of thumb: If you can smell it on yourself, you're wearing too much.

Hands & Nails

Many men turn up their noses at nail care, thinking rough, calloused hands are the mark of a real man.

Don't be silly. Manicurists have been working at good ol' boy barbershops for generations because groomed hands are nice to look at and even nicer to hold. What woman longs to be caressed by sandpaper and hangnails?

Hands are also extremely visible as we make our best points, conduct high-powered meetings, share important meals. Don't think no one will notice those bad nails. They will.

To keep hands in their best form, never bite your nails or cuticles. You can disfigure hands and nails permanently.

At the very least, keep a nailbrush and bar of soap near the bathroom sink and scrub beneath nails regularly. Trim fingernails weekly after a shower. Use a small clipper or scissors and trim to match the curve of the fingertip. A small pair of cuticle scissors can take care of hangnails.

DEAL KILLER
DIRTY NAILS

Dirt under a man's fingernails used to be a sign he was industrious. Today, it is a sign he is careless. If you think no one will notice a little dirt beneath your nails, you're wrong. You must keep them spotless at all times. Never clean them in public, however.

Even better, treat yourself to a professional manicure once a month. It will keep nails and hands in great shape. And, no, you won't emerge polished Poppy Red. A man's manicure is not like a woman's. No polish allowed, not even clear.

When the weather is cold, wear gloves. They protect hands and nails and look nice.

As for toenails, ditto with the brush and clippers or get a professional pedicure. How bad can it be having your feet massaged for forty-five minutes?

Also keep tough skin on feet from cracking with an occasional application of foot cream after your shower and/or rubbing on them in the shower with a pumice stone, available at the drugstore. No one will want to play footsie under the sheets otherwise.

Note that nail discoloration and lack of growth can signal fungal and other nasty disorders. If you notice anything strange, consult a physician or dermatologist.

The Body

There are many books devoted to health, diet, and exercise. We are not going to belabor the point here.

But we would be remiss if we didn't point out the importance of a well-toned, healthy body in today's competitive business world.

Not only will proper diet and exercise give you the energy you need to get where you're going physically and mentally, a fit body wears clothes well, exudes confidence, and reflects discipline. If you're packaging yourself for success, these elements are nonnegotiable.

Find something you like to do—running, walking, racquetball, swimming, tennis, yoga, cycling, pilates, martial arts—and establish a routine. Exercise doesn't have to be expensive. A forty-five-minute run and three sets of stomach crunches, push-ups, and lunges cost nothing and accomplish everything.

If you take up a sport requiring competition, make sure you have plenty of players. If it's a gym workout (recommended in addition to sport), make sure it's convenient and regular.

DEAL KILLER
SMOKING

With all we know today about the perils of inhaling tobacco, anyone who chooses to continue puffing looks pretty stupid and weak. Smoke makes you smell funky and forces you to seek company out behind buildings with others who share your addiction. It's not on that list of habits of highly successful people.

If you smoke, get help and quit. Until that liberating moment, always wash your hands and face before meeting nonsmokers. They can smell your foolishness even if you can't, and they don't find it attractive.

Early morning workouts are most efficient because the a.m. shower is already built in. Working out first thing also ensures it gets done before daily life can interfere. There's evidence morning exercise wards off late afternoon energy slumps.

Exercising at lunch works better for some. Still others look forward to it after hours to wind down and refresh. Beware that working out too late in the evening can sometimes interfere with sleep.

The goal is not to look like Mr. Universe. A thick neck and hulking trapeziums only make you look like a pinhead. The goal is healthy tone: defined arms and shoulders, strong chest, flat abs, narrow waist, firm butt, good posture.

There are many habits the successful male should avoid. Exercise, eating right, and maintaining a svelte body are not among them.

You'll need all the edge you can get.

Posture

Never underestimate the power of posture. It can give a shorter man stature or make a tall man look insignificant. How you carry yourself says much about who you are and affects how people react to you.

Whether sitting, standing, or walking, be aware of your posture. It should be neither ramrod straight nor so relaxed that your shoulders slump and your head bobs. Balance is what you want. Imagine you have a string tied to the crown of your head, pulling you skyward. Your head is balanced between your shoulders, neither forward nor back. Your neck is elongated right over your torso. Shoulders are down and slightly back, square over hips. Chest is forward. Stomach is in. Back is straight. Butt is tucked.

Good muscle tone is key to good posture. Poor muscle tone, and bad habits like hunching over a keyboard all day, work against good alignment. If your job creates bad habits, stretch often. Re-evaluate your workspace ergonomically. Work standing up.

Any time you sit, don't slouch on your tailbone. Sit on your butt and feel your thighs against the chair. Sit up straight with feet flat on the floor. Keep your head balanced on your shoulders—a good life lesson for all times.

GROOMING

There are two lists for what should be in your shaving kit when you travel. One constitutes essentials. The second subscribes to the Boy Scout motto: Be prepared.

Select from the second list according to anticipated need and/or destination.

ESSENTIALS

- shampoo and conditioner
- hair product (if you use one)
- razor
- shaving cream
- deodorant
- sunscreen with SPF 15 or higher
- comb or brush
- toothbrush
- toothpaste
- dental floss
- aspirin/ibuprofen
- Band-Aids
- prescription medication

GOOD IDEAS

- mouthwash
- tweezers
- Swiss army knife (but not in a carry-on bag, unless you'd like to donate it to airport security)
- nail clippers (also taboo in carry-on bags)
- cologne
- contact lens cleaner
- adapter kit
- cotton balls/cotton-tipped sticks
- foot powder
- nose-hair trimmer
- sewing kit
- skin lotion
- exfoliating scrub

- sleeping mask
- soap (in plastic bag or box)
- cold remedy
- throat lozenges
- antacid/anti-diarrhea medication
- eyedrops
- insect repellent
- moleskin for blisters
- medical emergency information (medication, physician's numbers)
- several sealable, empty plastic baggies to save buttons that come off, leaking shampoo bottles, etc.

CREDITS

PHOTOGRAPHY

Corbis

Page 53: *bottom left* Comstock

Page 88: Underwood & Underwood

Page 99: *top right* Wally McNamee

Page 114: *bottom left* Michael Kim

Page 114: *bottom right* Lisa O'Connor/ZUMA

Page 128: Bettmann

Page 134: Bettmann

Page 190: Bettmann

Page 191: Creasource

Page 192: Hans Klaus Techt/epa

Page 193: Reuter Raymond/Corbis Sygma

Page 195: Tim Graham

Page 216: Rufus F. Folkks

Page 266: *top left* Swim Ink 2, LLC

Page 275: Randy Faris

Getty Images

Cover and page 2: Stuart Dee

Page 4: *right* Double Exposure

Page 5: *left* altrendo images

Page 5: *center* Digital Vision

Page 44: Kent Larsson

Page 52: Stockbyte

Page 53: *top right* Erik Von Weber

Page 53: *bottom right* Andersen Ross

Page 60: *4th picture down* Beard & Howell

Page 83: *top* Image Source Black

Page 83: *bottom* William Howard

Page 90: Laurence Dutton

Page 101: Bernard Grilly

Page 103: *inset* Sergio Ranalli

Page 129: Wirelmage

Page 130: Erik Isakson

Page 132: Hiroyuki Matsumoto

Page 135: Peter Correz

Page 136: *top left* STOCK4B-RF

Page 136: *second from top* Per Magnus Persson

Page 136: *third from top* VCL/Spencer Rowell

Page 136: *fourth from top* Glen Allison

Page 136: *bottom left* Grant Faint

Page 137: Stockbyte

Page 138: Double Exposure

Page 139: *top left* Stockbyte

Page 139: *bottom right* Kevin Mackintosh

Page 140: Tetra Images

Page 142: *top left* Kristofer Dan-Bergman

Page 142: *right* Thomas Barwick

Page 143: Odilon Dimier

Page 144: Ross Anania

Page 145: Martin Barraud

Page 146: Stockbyte

Page 147: Nicholas Eveleigh

Page 148: *top* Ingram Publishing

Page 148: *bottom left* David Samuel Robbins

Page 149: ML Harris

Page 150: Marina Jefferson

Page 151: Ryan McVay

Page 152: Jean Louis Batt

Page 153: Christopher Robbins

Page 154: Stockbyte

Page 156: *top left* altrendo images

Page 156: *right* Herman Agopian

Page 157: John Cumming

Page 158: A.B.

Page 159: altrendo images

Page 160: Victoria Pearson

Page 161: *left* Andersen Ross

Page 161: *right* Adrian Weinbrecht

Page 162: *left* Glowimages

Page 162: *right* Sparky

Page 163: Medioimages/Photodisc

Page 164: *left* Panoramic Images

Page 164: *right* K. Sanchez/Cole Group

Page 165: altrendo nature

Page 166: Steve Mason

Page 167: Terry Williams

Page 168: Alan Thornton

Page 170: George Doyle

Page 171: Johner

Page 172: Larry Bray

Page 174: Flying Colours Ltd

Page 175: Steven Puetzer

Page 176: Tony Metaxas

Page 177: Art Vandalay

Page 182: Stewart Cohen

Page 189: *bottom left* Tariq Dajani

Page 189: *bottom right* Mike Powell

Page 194: Getty Images

Page 204: *left* Justin Pumfrey

Page 204: *right* Yellow Dog Productions

Page 205: *top* John Kelly

www.tomjames.com